Veryan Round Ho...

FROM
THE ROSELAND
TO
ST AUSTELL BAY

St Ewe Church, Walk 15

Trenowth Mill, Walk 17

First published 1997 by
LANDFALL PUBLICATIONS
Landfall, Penpol, Devoran, Truro, Cornwall TR3 6NW
Telephone 01872-862581

IMPORTANT NOTE

I have done my best to ensure that all the recommended routes are on public
rights of way, with a few unavoidable exceptions mentioned in the text, and
that they are all unobstructed. If you come across unexpected difficulties
please be patient, take the nearest practicable alternative route, and if
possible let me know about the problem. Please help farmers and other
landowners by leaving all gates as you found them, and by keeping dogs on
a lead when there are livestock nearby. Whilst every effort has been made to
ensure the accuracy of the directions and other information in this guide, no
responsibility can be taken by the author for any errors leading to action
being taken against users or readers of the book, or to disappointment, loss
or injury.

USING THE BOOK

The boxed note at the start of each walk description is intended to be read
before you set out; sometimes it would be useful to make preparations a day
or two in advance in order to get the most out of the walk. A star (*)
indicates that there is a note on this point. The directions, printed in **bold**
type, attempt to be very exact and explicit, but the maps are only rough
sketches, so I'd strongly recommend taking with you the relevant Ordnance
Survey maps. Landranger 204 (Truro, Falmouth & surrounding area) covers
most of the routes, but for the ones north of St Austell you need No. 200
(Newquay, Bodmin & surrounding area). Best of all for walkers is the
Pathfinder series; the sheets named "St Austell and Fowey", "St Newlyn East,
Indian Queens & St Dennis" and "Mevagissey and Tregony" are the relevant
ones.

COVER PHOTOGRAPHS BY BOB ACTON

Front: The valley path up towards Heligan from Mevagissey (Walk 6)
Back: The little waterfall at Hallane Beach,
with a glimpse of the cliffs to the west (Walks 7 & 9)

Typesetting, maps and illustrations by Bob Acton unless otherwise stated.
The maps are based upon the relevant Ordnance Survey Pathfinder maps
with the permission of The Controller of Her Majesty's Stationery Office
(Ref. 85033M). © Crown Copyright

Printed by the Troutbeck Press
and bound by R. Booth Ltd., Antron Hill, Mabe, Penryn, Cornwall

INTRODUCTION

The walks in *Around St Austell* and *Around Mevagissey* were originally intended to constitute one book. The two books I eventually made of them were published roughly simultaneously, and as luck would have it they have also both gone out of print at about the same time, so I have decided to take the opportunity to revert to my first plan and make one "bumper" volume.

Two of the original twenty walks have been omitted. The one based on Probus was never very satisfactory, since there were few outstanding "points of interest" along the way apart from Probus village itself and its magnificent church, and the scenery was not very memorable; but what made the decision to drop the walk inevitable was the new bypass, slicing right across the southern part of the route. Cutting the walk based on the Wheal Martyn China Clay Museum was much more debatable, but two problems with it decided the issue, namely the impediments in the footpath near Bojea Farm, and the fact that a certain amount of walking along a busy road was unavoidable. The Museum is, of course, a "must" for anyone interested in this region, and to carry out the full tour of the site constitutes a walk in itself.

There are a good many other changes - mostly for the better, I trust. The directions have been revised wherever difficulties have come to my attention, and many of the historical notes have been expanded. The more substantial of these notes are now indicated by a vertical line on the left, rather than being placed in "boxes" as before. Directions are now picked out in bold type. Leaving out the colour photos can hardly be claimed as an improvement, I admit, but doing so has helped me to keep the cover price reasonable, and reduces the weight of the book by a few milligrams.

Space is lacking to extol the delights of exploring this very varied small region. It's high time you went and found out for yourself!

ACKNOWLEDGEMENTS

As so often with books featuring a considerable amount of "industrial archaeology", I owe a debt of gratitude to Kenneth Brown and Charles Thurlow of the Trevithick Society for checking and where necessary correcting my references to mining, china clay and china stone. Several others have also given valuable help with the St Stephen walk, notably John Yeo of Terras Mill, John Hawkins of Hawkins Motors, and Courtenay Smale and Jack Goldsworthy of the Goonvean and Rostowrack China Clay Co. My thanks also go to Valerie Brokenshire for help with several walks in and around Tregrehan Mills, to the staff at Wheal Martyn Museum for their friendly advice, and to the management of English China Clays International for their sympathetic response to enquiries about access to several places in their ownership. I also want to thank the Revs. Michael Geach and John Rham for information about Veryan and St Ewe parishes, Maisie and Ivor Herring for giving my wife and me a guided tour of Heligan house and grounds, Colin Howlett (the Director of Marketing at the Lost Gardens of Heligan) for help with the note on Heligan, and Joanna Mattingly of the Royal Cornwall Museum for leading me to Charles Henderson's notes and supplying several interesting "snippets" about Tregony and other places. If I seem to have forgotten the help *you* gave, please forgive me - but it may be that you are mentioned in the main text, along with the many authors whose books, leaflets, articles and unpublished writings I have drawn upon.

CONTENTS

Below: *Mevagissey from Polkirt Hill (Walk 5)*

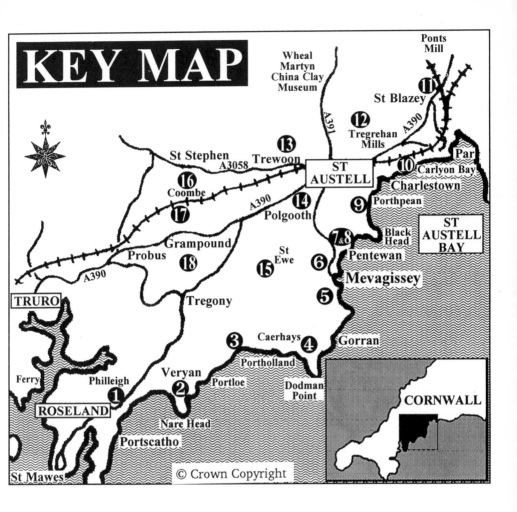

KEY MAP

Ponts Mill

Wheal Martyn China Clay Museum

St Blazey

⑪

⑫ Tregrehan Mills

A390

A391

St Stephen
A3058 Trewoon

⑬

ST AUSTELL

Par

⑩ Carlyon Bay

Charlestown

⑯
Coombe

⑰

A390

Polgooth

⑭

⑨ Porthpean

ST AUSTELL BAY

Grampound

Probus

⑱

St Ewe

⑮

Black Head

⑦⑧

Pentewan

⑥

A390

St TRURO

Tregony

Mevagissey

⑤

Caerhays

③

④

Gorran

Portholland

Ferry

Veryan

②

Portloe

Dodman Point

Philleigh

①

CORNWALL

ROSELAND

Nare Head

Portscatho

St Mawes

© Crown Copyright

WALK 1
PORTSCATHO, PENDOWER AND PHILLEIGH
A little over 8 miles. A shorter walk omitting Philleigh is also suggested.

Please don't let "8 miles" frighten you off this one: despite a few ups and downs, mainly along the coast, it's not at all exhausting, and we found it most enjoyable. We took about five hours over it, including a fairly long lunch stop at Philleigh. This is a region of gently rolling hills and long views, both coastal and inland; of picturesque villages and sturdy old farm buildings. A medieval church and an Iron Age fort are on or close to the route. A series of attractive bathing beaches is strung along this section of coast, and refreshments are available at two of them during the season; a pretty and cosy pub well-known locally for good food is very conveniently

placed a little over half-way along the route, and when you get back to Portscatho - if you time things well - there's the Plume of Feathers awaiting you. ("Everything that could be asked for in a pub" was the verdict on it in "The Complete Guide to Cornish Pubs".) If that's closed there are shops and seasonal cafés. The shorter route omits Pendower as well as Philleigh and amounts to about four-and-a-half miles. The inland paths are likely to require waterproof footwear (in fact you would be glad of wellies on the path approaching Rosevine: see section 8), and a stick to beat back brambles and other vegetation might prove valuable. The roads included on the route are all minor and usually very quiet ones, with the exception of about a quarter of a mile on the A3078. This is unavoidable at present because of a missing footbridge on a path.

To drive to Portscatho (unless you are using the King Harry Ferry), take the A3078 south from Tregony, turning left where signposted, first at Trewithian and then at Tregassa. Directions are given from the square in Portscatho, but during the season there is little or no long-stay parking down in the village, so use the car park on the left soon after the left turning at Tregassa. This gives you easy access to the coast path less than half a mile north of Portscatho, so if you don't want to visit the village you can shorten the walk slightly by turning left on reaching the cliff edge. There is another car park at Pendower Beach, point 2 in the directions.

WALK 1
PORTSCATHO

Gerrans/Portscatho can obviously be compared with Gorran/Gorran Haven and Levorrick/Porthilly (now combined as Mevagissey): in every case the church was built on high ground some way inland and gathered a village or "churchtown" around it, and a separate community developed at the nearest harbour. The churchtown was usually the older of the pair: Portscatho seems first to have been mentioned in documents in 1592, for example, nearly four centuries later than Gerrans, and Portscatho does not appear on Boazio's map (1597), whereas St Gerans is shown as quite a large village. Laurence O'Toole, however, believes that the two villages "must have grown at about the same pace." *(The Roseland: between River and Sea)* Certainly until this century they preserved very separate identities, even though Portscatho people had to go up to Gerrans for school as well as church. There was a definite boundary line, over which it was foolhardy for Gerrans children to venture after dark.

The name "Portscatho" means "harbour of boats" (specifically, large rowing-boats). Until 1891 there was no harbour wall, and such protection as there was was provided by ridges of rock near Pencabe Point. During the famous Great Blizzard of that year, however, some of those rocks had to be blasted to enable a wrecked ship, the German steamer *Carl Hirschberg*, to be towed off (with the aid of what a Portscatho lady called "carbolic jacks", according to an excellent but now scarce little book of local people's reminiscences compiled in the 1970s by the Vicar of Gerrans: *The Past in St Gerrans)*, and a short wall was built to replace the rocks. Later it was extended, but still proved a poor substitute, in the opinion of the older local fishermen. Hilary Thomson's *A History of Gerrans and Portscatho, 1700-1830* (1991) contains a wealth of human detail, painting particularly vivid pictures of the pilchard seining and the smuggling during that period. A map drawn in 1793 shows fish cellars lining almost the whole harbour - probably none too many, however, in view of catches like the one on 14 October 1809, totalling 1700 hogsheads: 51,000 fish. Ms Thomson writes of the evidence of hostility in the village towards the new "Preventive Waterguard" service set up in 1809 to combat smuggling, and tells of men arrested for lighting fires on shore as signals to smugglers. Even when Polsue was compiling his *Lake's Parochial History* (about 1865) the place was apparently still a byword in this respect: "Portscatha," he writes, "is a pretty and pleasantly situated village, and the change from a smuggling cove to a watering-place would be a most congenial one."

By the time Polsue was writing, the importance of fishing to Portscatho had been outstripped by the growth of boat building and especially by the busy merchant schooner trade: hence, as Hilary Thompson has pointed out in her latest book on Gerrans parish (1995), the preponderance of substantial terraced houses and "villas" in Portscatho rather than of fishermen's cottages as at Portloe and Mevagissey. For such reasons the seaside community here eventually became larger than the churchtown, and of course the 20th-century holiday industry has confirmed and quickened that process.

Polsue's wish has, I suppose, come true.

1 From Portscatho village square, either walk past the pub (built about 1756 and said to be the village's oldest surviving building) **or head towards the slipway, down River Street.** Formerly this was called Horse Road, reflecting the fact that it was much used by carts bringing up sand and seaweed for the farms. **Take the left turning, where there are coast-path acorn signs.** (Toilets are signposted further down River Street.) **Soon you are out of the village, and after a few steps up at the National Trust sign "Porthcurnick" you are walking along the edge of the low cliffs,** with a fine view ahead across Gerrans Bay to Nare Head and Gull Rock, the great bulk of the Dodman in the distance. **Near at hand is Porthcurnick Beach, and steps take you down to that.** (For the seasonal kiosk and toilets continue ahead up a few steps instead of going down the main flight of steps to the right.)

"Porthcurnick" or "Porth Cornick" means "little corner cove". So much sand was removed from this beach by farmers that the sea swept away a group of fishermen's cottages and an old lime kiln. A photograph from the 1890s showing the cottages is in Laurence O'Toole's *The Roseland, Between River and Sea* (1978), easily the best book about this area that I know of.

From the beach go a few yards up the slipway and turn right through the wooden gate with a NT sign, "Pednavadan". The coast path now heads east for a short distance, providing a good view of Portscatho with the spire of Gerrans church above and Greeb Point in the distance. At Pednvadan *(pen-tal-ban,* literally Brow-peak Head) is a small watch-house, manned in bad weather. Heading north again now, you can see Porthbean ("little cove") Beach with a hotel above, and the coast path takes you down to the beach. One of the steeper climbs on this route now follows, and there are a couple more ups and downs before you pass the dome-like green knoll known as the Round House and reach the cove called Creek Stephen. ("Creek" is a form of the Cornish *crug,* a barrow or burial mound. The Round House looks a very likely site for a barrow - and we are close to an undoubted prehistoric site here.)

This is the point at which I suggest you turn inland - following the sign to Curgurrell (another name containing "crug")- if you want to shorten the walk; and if you don't but are interested in seeing the Iron Age earthwork known as Dingerein Castle you might choose to make a short diversion here. The path runs beside Curgurrell Farm and brings you to the road. Continue ahead on that, and just before reaching the main road look over a farm gate on your left for a glimpse of the curved inner rampart of Dingerein Castle (*), close to the main road at the top end of the field. The high hedge beside the road is presumably part of the outer rampart.

DINGEREIN CASTLE

Like Resugga (Walk 17) and Carvossa (Walk 18), this is a Celtic Iron Age fort. It had two circular ramparts, but the outer one, which was a little over a hundred yards in diameter, has survived only at the north-western side (adjoining the road corner). The inner one is more complete, but again best-preserved in the north-western part. The ditches have gone completely. Old guide books such as *Murray's Handbook* of 1859 confidently state that an underground passage called the Mermaid's Hole links the earthwork with the shore. A Rector of Ruan Lanihorne at the end of the 18th century decided that the palace of the real or mythical Dark Age King Gerent (said with a hard G) must have been here, so he called the fort Dingerein, "Gerent's castle". The village and bay of Gerrans are also supposed to derive their name from Gerent, although it is possible that the church's patron saint (variously called Gerent, Geren, Gerance, Gerontius, etc.) was another person altogether. For more details about local legends which connect Gerent with prehistoric sites that originated a thousand years or more before his time, see the note on Carne Beacon in Walk 2. Another candidate for the site of Dingerein is the round at Carwarthen, north of St Just; but in fact there is no evidence that there was ever a place called Dingerein in Cornwall.

Return the same way to continue the full walk; otherwise go a few yards right on the main road, then cross and take the road going sharp left, which leads to the Merrose Farm caravan park and so can be quite busy in summer: hence the traffic lights. After a few yards turn left on to the signed bridleway, which runs for about half a mile and makes pleasant walking but can be very muddy towards the far end. At the main road continue ahead (or right) for about 50 yards, and then cross (with great care because of the closeness of a blind bend) to a small stone stile. Now pick up the directions at point 8.

The coast path continues along the cliff-edge. Beyond the NT sign, "Treluggan Cliffs", you see the Pendower Hotel ahead, and reach it after two more fairly gentle climbs. The coast path turns inland to avoid passing in front of the hotel, where coffee and food are available to non-residents. The road brings you down to the beach car park.

2 **Just before reaching the Pendower Beach House Hotel** (another source of refreshments during the season), **turn left up a rather narrow and steep path** where the stick I mentioned in the introductory note may come in handy. Look back for a pretty view of Pendower Beach. **After climbing a few steps, walk beside the hedge on your right, crossing a stile near the top of the hill; beyond a second stile, continue in the same line to a third one at the road.** Take care when negotiating the quite steep steps down on the far side, because this road tends to carry fast traffic. **Cross the road and the stile opposite, following the footpath sign to Treworthal. The path crosses this small field to another stile on the right side of a farm building.**

3 **Turn left on the minor road,** which takes you past several typical Cornish farms, with their mixtures of old and new buildings. Treworlas House is particularly attractive: a nicely restored former farmhouse which we guessed to be late Georgian in date. Names starting with "tre" (=farmstead, estate) usually end with a personal name (normally that of the original owner or farmer). Such is probably the case with Treworlas and the nearby Trevithick; "Treveans", however, means "small farm", and "Treworthal" "farm on watery ground" or possibly "thicket farm". In fact Treworthal is a hamlet rather than a farm, and a very pretty little place, with its thatched cottages, red phone kiosk and Queen Victoria post-box. (We were told that snails have taken up residence in there, so the villagers avoid posting their mail in the evenings!) Until at least 1753 Treworthal had a windmill; it stood on the site of a prehistoric burial ground.

Treworthal

4 Just before the last thatched cottage, take the footpath on the left, signed to White Lane and Philleigh. The path, mostly a sunken track with a few stiles, quite soon brings you to another road, opposite a former chapel now converted and extended to form a handsome residence with a fine view including Philleigh Church and a glimpse of the River Fal at Ardevora. The stack of the Trelonk brickworks can be seen. (For details, see Walk 8 in the latest edition of *Around the Fal.)* **Turn left. The road runs down through White Lane; just beyond the houses there, take the footpath on the right, signed to Philleigh. It is just to the left of a metal farm gate, and starts at a wooden stile.** This path tends to get rather overgrown, and if that proves a problem you could continue to Philleigh on the road instead. **The path brings you into the village** beside Polglaze ("green pool") Farm, whose small hill of black plastic is perhaps the least charming sight in Philleigh. On the left is the early Georgian or Queen Anne Glebe House, which till 1939 was the Rectory, was requisitioned by the Royal Engineers in the run-up to D-Day, and is now a private residence again after a period as a guest house and restaurant. **Go on past the farm, the little school building and the church.**

PHILLEIGH

An old name for the village is Eglosros, "the church in the moorland" or possibly "the Roseland church". The manor, of which nothing now survives, is named "Eglosos" or "Egleshos" in the Domesday Book. The church is dedicated to an unknown saint called Fily; the "Ph" had appeared by 1597, when Baptista Boazio drew his fascinating map of the Fal estuary, and the "eigh" improvement seems to be a later Anglicisation on the model of

"Leigh", meaning woodland, clearing or meadow. The castellated church tower is one of the oldest parts of the building, dating from the 13th century. Inside, the font is probably of the same period, and the south arcade ("low and lovely", says Betjeman) was built about two centuries later. Not much else escaped the attentions of the Victorian restorers in 1867: according to Betjeman they "almost rebuilt" the church. The village now seems a very sleepy little place - or rather, it would be but for the popularity of the Roseland Inn. A century or more ago it presumably had more life of its own, judging by the fact  that "A substantial school premises was built adjoining the churchyard in 1860" *(Lake's Parochial History);* it is now the parish hall, and the few local children are bussed to Gerrans or Tregony. The road through Philleigh must once have been a busy trade route linking West Cornwall with the important port of Tregony via the King Harry Ferry. According to the King Harry Steam Ferry Company's centenary booklet (1988), the road was also part of the Pilgrims' Way to St Michael's Mount. Presumably in medieval or Tudor times travellers were more likely to patronise the inn than are the modern car-drivers trying to catch the ten-to or the ten-past.

For more about Philleigh, see the well-written booklet by Norman & Joyce Hicks, *Philleigh in the Roseland* (date/publisher not given).

(There is a signed path to the right just before the church, which leads down to a beautiful and peaceful spot beside the River Fal. It makes a worthwhile little diversion, amounting to slightly above a mile there and back, but you are likely to need wellies. The route is clearly indicated with yellow waymarks all the way. The earlier part, after you have crossed a couple of stiles, is on farm tracks; then you have to walk diagonally across two fields. Towards the end, where the path dips into woodland, it becomes a sunken lane wide enough for carts to bring coal and other goods from the riverside, where there is a small beach but no sign of a quay. Laurence O'Toole speculates that this may have been "the way the wandering footsteps of St Filius arrived, fourteen hundred years ago.")

On the left just before the picture-postcard Roseland Inn, reputed to date from the 16th century but stated by Norman & Joyce Hicks to date from 1715, notice what Betjeman describes as "a little Regency Gothick cottage"; it looks rather like two Veryan round houses linked as Siamese twins. "The shed adjoining the inn," say the Hicks, "was formerly the poor house." Beyond the pub on the right is Court Farm, whose name is perhaps a clue to the site of the old manor house (compare St Stephen and Lanreath, where the manors were called Court, probably in reference to manorial court-leets).

Continue along the road for about half a mile. (Walking along this road requires some care, even though it is rarely if ever busy: see the final comment in my note on Philleigh.)

5 Where it bends right, continue ahead along a narrow but tarmacked lane marked "Unsuitable for motors". The truth of this warning emerges after you have passed Trelissa, when it gradually deteriorates to a fairly rough and perhaps muddy track. Gerrans church spire can be seen, and at one point you get a glimpse of the Percuil River. **At the T-junction turn left. Soon the track descends - quite steeply at one point - to a ford and footbridge.** Lawrence O'Toole describes this "tiny lane" as the only one in Roseland which "has preserved its medieval simplicity." The ford is called Trelissa Watering: horses were tethered to the ring on the bridge while they drank. **Finally a short climb brings you to a road.**

6 Turn left there. The road climbs past Lanhoose ("grey valley") and at the top of the hill the sea comes back into view. The farm here is Tregaire.

TREGAIRE

The name derives from *tre-ker*, "farm of the fort or round". Tregaire Barton stands on a hill and has the sort of wide view usually associated with hill forts, but there is no sign of one here. More surprisingly, there appears to be no relic - not even a carved stone in a farm hedge - of the Chapel of the Holy Cross which was consecrated by Bishop Bronescombe of Exeter in 1463. Tregaire or Tregear was one of the great episcopal manors, given to the Church by King Egbert in the 9th century and listed in Domesday as Tregel. At that time it boasted the unusually large number of sixty teams of oxen (eight to a team). Its lands included the whole of the Roseland peninsula apart from the small manor of Eglosros (see the note on Philleigh), plus St Michael Penkivel parish and parts of Ruan Lanihorne and Feock parishes, and "High Rents" were paid to it from estates as far afield as St Keverne, St Erth and Mevagissey. The map of Tregear Manor drawn by the great Cornish historian Charles Henderson is reproduced in Laurence O'Toole's book. By the end of the 13th century most of the estates had been sold or let as sub-manors. Medieval Bishops of Exeter frequently visited until about 1450; after that, Tregaire became a mere barton, the chapel was eventually desecrated, and now "The farmhouse itself has hardly any ancient features". ("History of the Parish of Gerrans" (1938), included with Canon Doble's account of S.Gerent, recently republished and available in local shops.) Perhaps the only clear sign now of its former importance, apart from a mass of old documents, is the fact that it still has (or had in 1978, says O'Toole) more land than any other Roseland farm.

7 At the main road there should be a footpath straight on, but a combination of barbed wire and a missing footbridge have made it unusable except to the truly intrepid rambler. I have pointed out this problem to the County Footpaths Officer, and in the hope that one day the path will be restored I have shown it with small dots on my map. As things stand, however, **you have to turn left and brave the traffic on the A3078.** The verge on the far side is helpful, but ironically it disappears where most needed, at the right-hand bends. **Continue for about a quarter of a mile,** though it will probably seem longer.

8 Don't miss the rather small and somewhat overgrown stone stile on the right, just before a sharp right-hand bend. Cross it and walk along the centre of the field, heading towards the distant spire at Gerrans. The path has a series of stiles, several of which make life difficult by being brambly, awkwardly high, surrounded by mud or all three. **After the fourth stile (counting the one at the road as the first) you need to go slightly left to a wooden step-stile and then follow the direction indicated by the yellow arrow, diagonally to the right. At the field corner go through the metal farm gate, walk beside the hedge on your left, and turn left through a second gate just before the farm buildings.** This is Pollaughan, "pool of the oxen". **The right of way runs beside the farmhouse and along the tarmacked drive to the road. Cross that with care and continue ahead on the path signed "Rosevine". Walk almost straight ahead, but slightly to the right, towards the bungalow. Cross the stile behind a small wooden gate and go down a little to the left to cross a stream.** The rather elaborate stile here is made awkward with some wooden bars, and then you are faced with a very muddy patch, churned up by cattle. With the aid of a few stones and bits of wood we managed to cross it more-or-less unscathed, but I can imagine this becoming a real morass during rainy spells. After that little adventure, **walk up the slope to join the road via a stile and a fenced path just to the right of the bungalow.**

9 Turn right. The road runs gently downhill among the houses and hotels of Rosevine - a pretty name which apparently derives from the Cornish *ros-breyn,* putrid moor. I hasten to add that the name seems to have no relevance nowadays. Laurence O'Toole writes of the remains of a tiny Iron Age settlement found in 1958 at Rosevine by a bungalow owner digging his garden: pottery, a quern for corn-grinding, part of a stone hammer, and remains of shellfish, pigs and sheep. **Soon you are back at Porthcurnick Beach, and from there you will know the way back to the car park or down into Portscatho.**

Portscatho - from an old photograph

WALK 2
VERYAN, PORTLOE AND NARE HEAD
About nine miles - but several shorter versions are suggested,
ranging from about four-and-a-half to seven-and-a-half miles.

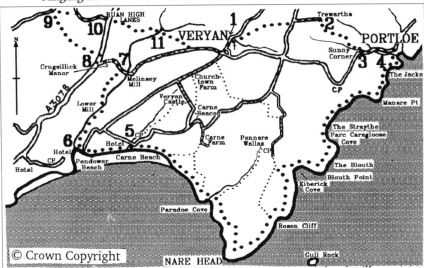

© Crown Copyright

This walk is based on one of Cornwall's loveliest inland villages and
also includes one of the most unspoilt fishing havens. The inland
walking is pleasant and mostly away from roads; the coastal section is
spectacular and in places quite strenuous. You will need to be prepared
for mud, and there are one or two places on the cliffs which require
particular care. The path running through the valley above Pendower
Beach is sometimes rather overgrown. Veryan and Portloe both have
public toilets, pubs and shops, and the shop at Portloe also serves coffee,
teas and other refreshments during the season; there is a general store at
the filling station at Ruan High Lanes. There are several good beaches
along the way, but some of them are accessible only by scrambling. If you
are planning to take a dog, be sure to keep it on a lead, especially along
the coast path, where farmers' notices warn of the drastic measures taken
against dogs that worry sheep. A bewilderingly large number of
attractive circular routes around Nare Head could be devised, especially
now that the National Trust has opened up new paths, or made old ones
available to the public, and there are car parks at Portloe, close to Nare
Head near Pennare Wallas Farm, and at Carne and Pendower beaches, so
that you can quite easily plan your walk to enable you to have a pub lunch
at Veryan or Portloe, for example. A combination of the National Trust's
"Coast of Cornwall" Leaflet No. 20 and the OS "Pathfinder" map should
enable you to work out even more routes if you need them!

Veryan (*) is signposted from the A3078 south of Tregony. There is usually
plenty of space for parking near the school and public toilets, opposite the
main entrance to the church.

VERYAN

"A Cornish delight in a leafy dell", it was called by Arthur Mee, and Betjeman describes it as a "mild tropic garden". It is best known for its five round houses, four of them thatched, built early in the 19th century by a wealthy and vigorous Vicar, Jeremiah Trist. (Not that he needed to be particularly wealthy to do so: apparently one pair of round houses cost under £70 to build.) The cross on the top of each perhaps helped to encourage the local tradition that the purpose of the circular shape was to deny the devil any corner to hide in, or to fool him into being unable to find the entrance to the village. Christine North, in her excellent history of Veryan, is sceptical about this and other legends about them, remarking simply that "The Houses were built to a "rustic" design fashionable at the time and enhanced the appearance of Trist's extensive property in the village." The most impressive example of that was (and is) Parc Behan, the house near Veryan Green, north of the churchtown, which he built for himself about 1810. It now belongs to the National Trust and has been divided into flats. Many of the trees in the "leafy dell" date from the time when the Trists were landscaping the village. For a detailed account of the three generations of the Trist family who dominated life in Veryan from 1773 to 1869, see Christine North's article in the 1980 *Journal of the RIC.*

The principal Domesday manor of Veryan was Elerky or Elerkey, whose owners have included the Lercedekne family, associated with the building of the castle at Ruan Lanihorne (see *Around the Fal,* Walk 7), and the Tregians of Golden (see Walk 18 in this book). The manor house has long gone, but the McLeod Water Garden may perhaps mark the site of its swannery: the name Elerky means swan or swanpool.

The church includes Norman features, with 13th- and 15th-century additions; it was restored in the 1840s and again in 1897-8, but less harshly than many other Cornish churches. A wall monument worth looking

for is that of Admiral Kempe, who sailed with Captain Cook and was at Quebec with Wolfe. A descendant of his, who made or inherited a fortune from a cough mixture called "Liquafruta", bequeathed money to build and maintain a group of houses in Veryan for the widows of Cornish seamen.

The dedication of the church to St Symphorian probably explains the name of the village: by the 16th century the name was being written as "Severian", and that eventually turned into "St Veryan". Symphorian was a Burgundian, martyred in the 3rd century; various theories have been put forward as to how his name came to be linked with this place. Some say that the saint behind the name is actually Berriona, a 6th-century Irish virgin who is supposed to have cured the son of King Geraint when he was paralysed. (See the notes on Carne Beacon in this walk and Dingerein Castle in Walk 1.) Veryan's Holy Well, now dry, stands opposite the church; it was restored in 1912.

1 The walk begins just to the left of the war memorial as you look towards the church. There is a Public Footpath sign (Portloe via Trewartha), but it may be hidden by leaves. The path passes through the small memorial gardens with their pond; after a kissing gate you pass through a children's play area. Cross the bridge at the far right-hand corner of this. After the stile, make for another stile you will see beside a small wood to your right, but do not cross it. Instead, walk on up the field, heading for the top-left corner, where you will find a small iron gate. (The large house to your left, by the way, is Parc Behan, mentioned in the note on Veryan.) **Go through the gate, over the stile on the other side of the patch of woodland, and continue straight on across the field, aiming for the farm buildings. After the 7-bar gate, the lane brings you past a former Methodist chapel to a road. Here turn left and then immediately right, still following the public footpath to Portloe.** The headland now coming into view on the horizon is the Dodman.

2 At the farm entrance (Trewartha Hall) turn left through the metal gate, and when you come to two more gates go through the one on the left. Keep by the hedge on your right till you reach the kissing gate - a tight squeeze if you've got a back-pack, and perhaps even if not! Now head for the buildings in the valley bottom and go through the gate on the left by the first cottage. You then pass through the garden in front of the cottage. This is "Sunny Corner", even in the rain. Up to the right are the remains of a watermill, but the sluice gate just to your left as you approach the road, and the millstone decorating the entrance to Spear-Point opposite, are fairly recent imports.

3 Cross the bridge on the road and turn left, down past the Ship Inn into Portloe (*). The long, low old building on the right just below the Ship was, the pub's landlord told me, used as a coal store within living memory, but may possibly have been a pilchard cellar before that. **At the bottom fork right** for the Lugger Hotel (which also offers bar food, but only during the season), the public toilets and the small harbour.

PORTLOE

The name probably means "harbour of an inlet". Despite its popularity as a place to visit, Portloe has kept much of its character as a fishing village, mainly, I suppose, because there's so little room for "development" in what Liz Luck calls its "cramped and dramatic" situation, huddled around its tiny harbour at the bottom of steep hills.

The original lifeboat house of 1869 was replaced by All Saints Church; the later one, more conveniently situated down by the water, became an infants' school four years after the lifeboat station was closed in 1887, and later the village institute. The fish cellars have gone - some of them stood on what is now The Lugger's car park -, but two limekilns are near the church (the left-hand one is particularly well preserved, but unfortunately seems to double as the village litter-bin), and there are remains of others up by The Ship. Which of these kilns was the scene of an accident reported in *The West Briton* in July 1841, I don't know: "On Sunday, the 4th instant, a little girl, about five years old, daughter of Mr Paine, of the Coast Guard, at Portloe, was unfortunately burnt to death, by attempting to take a roasted potatoe from a lime-kiln."

In 1855 the village had two inns: The Ship, locally nicknamed "The Drinking Kitchen", rebuilt in 1904 after a fire; and the New Inn, which, I believe, became The Lugger.

Portloe shares with most of the other south coast villages a long history of smuggling, dating back at least to the 17th century when the famous smuggler and pirate Robert or Robin Long lived at Veryan, and still thriving in 1843 (I mean the smuggling, not Robin Long, who is said to have ended his days hanging in chains at Bessybeneath, where the road to Veryan leaves the A3078) when the coastguards recovered over forty barrels of liquor which had been anchored to the sea bed: the anchor-ropes got caught up in a fisherman's hooks.

4 The coast path heading south and west leaves Portloe a few yards below the toilets. *(An alternative way up to the cliffs, avoiding The Jacka and a rather uncomfortably steep little downward slope, is the path that starts beside the toilets.)* **You now climb The Jacka,** which provides you with fine views over the village, but it's especially here that you need to tread carefully: the path goes perilously close to the edge just past the seat. **After a steep little drop, followed by quite a steep climb, bear left where the path forks, keeping to the cliff edge.** At Manare Point, where there are two stiles in quick succession, you will see Parc Camels and Parc Caragloose Coves below you. "Parc" means "field". "Camels", the name of a hamlet nearby, means "curved shore" or "crooked cliff", and "Caragloose" appears in various forms along the Cornish coast: Carrick Lûz (Lizard) and Cataclews (near Padstow), for example. It means "grey rock". The island ahead has a name even more frequently found: Gull Rock. It achieved fame and glory during the 1950s as a set in a film of *Treasure Island* (the same film included other scenes shot at Pill Creek, Feock); before that Gull Rock was perhaps best known for the wreck of the German ship *Hera* in 1914. The nineteen who died are buried in Veryan churchyard. After you pass the pines of Broom Parc House (used, I believe, as the setting for much of the TV film of Mary Wesley's *The Camomile Lawn),* the path winds down, and at the lowest point you are only a few feet above the rocks. These are called The Straythe, referring to the stream you have just crossed (Cornish, *streyth,* stream). The Straythe was the scene of a shipwreck during the great blizzard of 1891. The *Dundella* was carrying a cargo of fruit, and if you are given a painful bite as you pass it may be that you have been attacked by what locals used to call "a Dundella fly". People believed the flies hatched from rotten pineapples left on board, and plagued the area ever since. Bites or no bites, it's a hard slog now up to the cliffs known as The Blouth (probably from the Cornish *blogh,* bald, bare). At the southern end is Blouth Point, overlooking Kiberick Cove, with a beach that looks fairly inaccessible from the cliffs. "Kiberick" may derive from the Cornish word for timber - perhaps a hint of a long-forgotten shipwreck.

For the shortest way back to Veryan, take one of the paths inland to the National Trust's car park near Pennare Wallas (Lower Pennare farm), which is visible from the coast path as you approach from above Kiberick. The first is the shortest of all: simply take the path on the right after following the coast path round to the head of the valley above Kiberick Cove. Secondly, you could continue to Rosen ("little promontory") Cliff and take the track north from there, with a cattle grid at the start. You can recognise this place by the very sheer cliff on your left, with Gull Rock at about its closest. Beside the coast path are a disused World War II bunker and (to quote the NT leaflet) "the ventilators of an underground Royal Observer Corps station". I wonder what they observe down there. A third possibility - and the best - is to go on around Nare Head to Paradoe Cove and walk up the delightful wooded valley to the car park from there. Beyond the car park you continue north for about half a mile on a surfaced road, and then take the footpath signposted to Veryan, on the left where the road bends sharply right. After crossing the stile, go by the hedge on the left, over a fence-like stile, then across to the hedge opposite. Walk with that on your left; when you come to a gap with a low wooden fence cross to the next field and go on with the hedge on your right. Cross a track, go through a small gate and continue beside the hedge to the corner, where stiles help you up and over a high hedge. Turn left on the road. After the farm entrance, cross the stile on the right. The path crosses the field, cutting off the right-hand corner. Cross the double stile and walk down the long field, roughly in the centre, to a further stile; then go straight on, with a wire fence on your right. At the road turn right for the centre of Veryan.

From Nare Head you have fine views of the Dodman in the east (and as far as Rame Head, near Plymouth, in really clear conditions) to the Manacles and Lowland Point in the west, with Portscatho across Gerrans Bay in the middle distance. As with Nare Point on the other side of the Helford, the name merely means "headland", being a shortened form of Penare or Pennare, the names of nearby farms. Nare Head has belonged to the National Trust since 1931; until then it was the property of the Williams family of Caerhays. Another quite strenuous section of the coast path follows, particularly at Paradoe Cove (pronounced "Perarda"), a beautiful spot, complete with stream and a lonely building which estate agents would describe as an ideal opportunity for the handyman. The NT leaflet tells the story of the fisherman called Mallet who built it early in the 19th century. A cave nearby is called Tregagle's Hole, one of many Cornish places

The ruins of Mallet's cottage at Paradoe Cove

associated with the doomed, wandering spirit who howls or moans in anguish among the rocks and on the bleak moors - a spirit represented in the mythologies of many lands, but in Cornwall given the name of an actual person, a wicked steward from Trevorder, near St Breock. (His family was called Tregeagle, but the spelling "Tregagle" shows how the name is said.) (See *Around Padstow,* Walk 5.) Just beyond Paradoe Cove is a spot I remember from a walk here one May, when there was a breathtaking display of multicoloured flowers, with bluebells, campion, foxgloves, the dark red spikes of docks, the tall yellow heads of wild cabbage, the whites of stitchwort and cow parsley, plus the inevitable dandelions and buttercups, all shining out through the tall, feathery grasses and the bright new fronds of bracken. **Where the path divides, keep left for the cliff path to Carne Beach,** *but fork right, following the yellow arrow on the acorn post, to return to Veryan via Carne Beacon, thus completing a round walk of just over six miles. At the T-junction turn right. After passing among the buildings of Carne Farm, continue ahead at the road, and where the road bends left still go on in the same direction, crossing the stile signposted Churchtown Farm. The path goes along the left side of the burial mound on top of Carne Beacon (*) and then straight on, crossing two stiles. The official path cuts across the field, reaching the road via a stile just to the left of the farm buildings. Turn right at the road, and you soon enter Veryan between two of its famous round houses.*

CARNE BEACON

This is one of the most impressive prehistoric remains in Cornwall, a Bronze Age round barrow of unusually large proportions in a very commanding position on a hill 370 feet above sea level. ("Carne" itself means barrow, and it has been used as one of the chain of beacons along the south coast.) Not surprisingly, there is an ancient tradition that it was the burial place of a king, specifically the 6th- or 8th-century King Gerent, Gerennius or Geraint, after whom Gerrans and Dingerein Castle (at Curgurrel, north of Portscatho: Walk 1) are said to be named. Excavation revealed a stone burial chest but none of the rich grave goods that might be expected of a royal interment, let alone the golden ship with silver oars that the legend claims was buried with him. The barrow, of course, predates Gerent by something between 1600 and 3000 years.

5 The coast path emerges on to a road just above Carne Beach. There are toilets in the National Trust car park.

Yet another possible and worthwhile route back to Veryan is via Veryan Castle.

This earthwork, probably the remains of an Iron Age settlement, has a very unusual setting: instead of the usual hilltop or promontory site, it was built on a slope which had to be excavated in order to provide a level platform, with a steep drop on the west side. The remains of a bank and ditch can be seen on the uphill side. The site has not been the subject of an archaeological "dig", so nothing is known about the dwellings which presumably existed, not only within the main enclosure but possibly also outside it, since there are traces of outer defences on the east side. Local names for the site are Veryan Rings and the Ringarounds.

For this, take the permissive path which starts at the inland end of the NT car park. After crossing the stile to the right of the gate, follow the line indicated by the signpost: up to the hedge on the right and over the stile to the right of the 5-bar gate. Now the flat platform of the earthwork is to your left, commanding a fine view of the valley and the bay, with a glimpse of the Goonhilly Downs dishes on the skyline. Beyond the earthwork the path crosses a stone stile and runs beside the hedge on your right. From here there is a good view left to "china-clay country", and close at hand to the right is the barrow that marks the top of Carne Beacon. Turn left on the road and right at the T-junction for Veryan. .

For the longer walks, continue along the coast to Pendower Beach: you can go along the foreshore if the tide allows, although the cliff-edge path, the victim of erosion, has recently been repaired and brought back into use. Above the beaches is the Nare Hotel, and above that Gwendra ("white sands") Farm, now holiday accommodation. Gwendra is one of the few places in Cornwall where limestone has been quarried in useful quantities. Presumably it was burnt in the two kilns at Pendower whose ruins have survived. "Pendower" means "foot of the water", referring probably to the stream beside which the next part of the walk runs.

6 Don't go as far as the Pendower Beach Hotel, but from the beach car park take the bridleway up the valley, just to the right

of the stream. **At Lower Mill (Melinsey Cottages) go through the courtyard and over the footbridge.** The path continues quite steeply up through the woodland. This part of the walk tends to be overgrown, with a fair proportion of nettles, and a stout pair of trousers would be an advantage. **The path reaches a road at Melinsey Mill,** whose name means "mill-house". This and the Lower Mill were the manor mills of Elerky: see the note about Veryan. The ruins of Melinsey Mill ("surely one of the smallest mills in Cornwall", according to D.E.Benney's *Cornish Watermills)* are a few yards along the road to the right; its waterwheel - made at Harris and Polmear's City Foundry, Truro, in 1882 - is still in place.

7 One last choice of route presents itself here: **either turn right and return to Veryan on this narrow and in places steep road** (it carries a moderate amount of traffic, so you need to take care); **or for a route that is mainly on paths, passing through pleasant but not outstandingly attractive countryside, turn left.** This soon brings you past Crugsillick Manor, whose name means "Sillick's barrow": the OS map indicates a tumulus close by, on the right side of the road.

8 **At the main road turn right, then take the footpath on the left, signposted to Treworgan, which starts at a gate less than a hundred yards on. Follow the line of the hedge straight on, and go through the second gate or gap on the right. Now head for the farm - not the closest group of buildings, to the left, but the older-looking ones with a lane leading towards them. Go down to the field corner by the lane. To get on to the lane you may need to step over a low wire fence at the field entrance. The lane takes you past the farm and brings you to a crossroads.**

9 **Now take the footpath on the right; it cuts diagonally across the field to a stile near the far right-hand corner. Turn right at the road, which brings you to Ruan High Lanes,** where there is a garage with a shop where you can buy provisions.

10 **At the T-junction turn left, signposted Truro, and then immediately right on to the footpath to Veryan, which starts as a narrow path up some steps and over a decaying wooden stile. Keep the hedge on your left at first, but after the second stone stile cross the stile on your left and continue with the hedge on your right. The path goes down into the valley, keeping left of the woodland.**

11 **After crossing the stream by a slate bridge, climb the steps and go straight up over the ridge of the field to where you will see a wrought-iron gate. Go through that and make for the three trees at the field corner. Here a stile returns you to the road. Turn left for Veryan.** The New Inn will probably be a welcome sight!

Postscript: For entertaining personal reminiscences of life in Veryan, focusing mainly on the 1940s, look out for two little books by Frank Symons: *Veryan Memories* (1992) and *Were they the Good Old Days?* (1995), both published by the Lodenek Press.

WALK 3
PORTHOLLAND AND PORTLOE,
with a possible extension to
CAERHAYS CHURCH AND CASTLE

About four and a half miles,
or a little over seven miles with the extension.
Could be done as two separate walks.

If Portloe has esaped the worst consequences of being a magnet to holiday-makers, Portholland, despite its attractive setting and good beach, miraculously seems to be completely unspoilt by tourism - though it does at least acknowledge its existence by providing toilets and a car park. There is also a tiny shop.

The inland route that starts this walk takes you through typical Cornish coastal farming country, and the going here is easy, apart from the initial long climb. Nearly a mile is on roads, normally very quiet, although there may be quite a lot of traffic on the road up from Portloe during the season. The path south of Cruggan has sometimes been ploughed and not reinstated, so good, watertight footwear is advisable. At Portloe you will find more toilets, another shop, this time doubling as a café, and two pubs, though one of those (The Lugger) is likely to be closed out of season. The Ship is a little way up the hill on the far side of the village.

The walk back to Portholland along the coast is a fine one, but be prepared for several long, steep climbs. A couple of short stretches are, in fact, unusually steep, and might be quite hard to manage if you were walking in the opposite direction and had to descend them. The walk from Portholland to Caerhays is interesting and makes a good contrast. It starts with a long inland climb, but the return coastal walk is comparatively easy.

You could shorten this walk in several ways: by omitting the church, or the castle at Porthluney Cove, or even both! An attractive possibility would be to start, reasonably early in the morning, with the Caerhays walk (point 7) and continue to Portloe in time for lunch plus a rest to recharge your batteries for the rigours (and splendours) of the coast.

22

WALK 3

The directions start at the car park in East Portholland. To drive there from St Austell, take the A390 west towards Truro and fork left just beyond Hewas Water towards Tregony (B3287). The winding and narrow road that eventually reaches the coast at East Portholland is the second left turning from that. From Truro, leave the A390 just beyond Tresillian, taking the A3078 Tregony/St Mawes road. About 2 miles beyond Tregony follow the sign (left) for Veryan; then it's first left, first right and first left again. This road brings you to the coast at West Portholland, where there is a small parking space overlooking the beach, but for the main car park, toilets and shop turn sharp right, down into East Portholland.

PORTHOLLAND

Portholland consists of little more than a chapel, a smallholding and a few fishermen's cottages around two small coves, each with its stream. The smallholding, complete with pond, ducks, geese, hens and doves, still seems to be thriving, but there's little if any fishing now: despite the lack of obvious commercialisation (a result, I presume, of the influence of the Williams family of Caerhays), the hamlet is probably just as dependent on the holiday business as others along the Cornish coast. In the early 1960s John Betjeman formed the impression that the cottages are "summer hide-outs"; if it was true then it's hardly likely to be less so thirty years later. East Portholland's Methodist chapel, now 110 years old, is sadly neglected-looking and not as yet "converted", but the one overlooking the other cove is still in use. The name is pronounced *Port-holland* (rather than *Porth-olland*). An old version of it is Portallan; possibly the main stream was once known as the Allan or Allen, which is certainly found elsewhere in Cornwall as a river name. The River Allen, for example, flows through Truro, and Alan is the old name for the River Camel.

1 From the main car park in Portholland, you could cross the beach to the coast path westwards at low tide; it is not advisable to try scrambling along the rocks and concrete sea defences below the cliffs: a notice at the other end warns that the cliffs are very unstable. **Otherwise walk back up the road past the toilets, turning sharp left to West Portholland and left again at the Methodist Chapel.** Notice the well-preserved pair of limekilns, behind the lifebuoy and an old winch. Cross the stream and climb the steps on the right. This part of the coast path heads a little way inland, climbing quite steeply for several hundred yards with a valley down to your right.

2 When you come to a signpost, leave the coast path by continuing straight ahead on the Public Byway to Morvah. Here the path is being invaded by Japanese knotweed, a very rampant plant which seems to thrive on most herbicides. **At the bungalows, bear left along the tarmacked lane.**

3 At the road, go left and continue for about half a mile, ignoring the left turning to Tregenna. (The sign advertising Veryan Vineyard might well, however, tempt you to go and investigate. To check opening times, ring 01872-501404. From Tregenna there is a footpath to Cruggan, so you would not need to return to the road.)

Limekilns at Portholland

4 Turn left to Cruggan farm, one of the many place names in Veryan parish which derives from the Cornish *cruc,* barrow or hillock. In many cases, though not all, this indicates a prehistoric burial mound; none is marked on the "Pathfinder" map here, but such features have often been ploughed out, and this is the more likely at Cruggan because the name probably comes from *criggan,* the diminutive form of the word. **Follow the concrete drive round to the right, through the gate into the farmyard. Bear left, passing between the farmhouse and the other main building; here another farm gate, with an old footpath sign beside it, brings you to a lane. Soon you cross a wall by steps into a field where the path may have been ploughed**

up. A sign directs you to head for the bungalow, that is, the nearest building; this means crossing the field, heading slightly to your right. At the left side of the bungalow there is a kissing gate which brings you to a road.

5 Turn left and continue down the road into Portloe. There is a note about the village in Walk 2. Unless you have done that walk already or plan to, it would be worth climbing to the top of "The Jacka", the cliff above the harbour on the far side, for the fine view of the village.

6 The coast path back to Portholland is clearly signposted. It takes you past the Methodist Chapel and a beautifully restored mill. The waterwheel has gone, but the leat, complete with sluice gate, is still there, and you can see where a channel has been cut for it in the rocks below. The path runs in front of a row of cottages, then up steps, past "The Flagstaff", and behind the coastguard lookout hut. One might guess that the fishermen's "huer's hut" was at The Flagstaff; it also looks like the ideal site for the Watch House that was built for the preventive officers at Portloe: see Mary Waugh's *Smuggling in Devon & Cornwall 1700-1850.* The National Trust's leaflet, however, refers to "an early type of coastguard lookout". As you descend from there, the view ahead embraces Caragloose Point, Porthluney Cove, Hemmick Beach and the Dodman. After a steepish climb with steps, the path descends to Caragloose Point, where the "grey rocks" almost form an island, and a complete island, Shag Rock, is just offshore. From here you can see Manacle Point, fifteen or more miles south west on the Lizard peninsula. The long and in places steep climb that follows takes you to Carn Pednathan, probably meaning "birds'-tor head". Now it's down again, through an attractive little wooded patch, to the valley and cove below Tregenna, with its two footbridges. The beach is still a little way below and not easy to reach, but the OS map names "Cellar Rock" down there, which suggests that it was a place for landing fish or contraband or both. Once more the path climbs, this time heading inland, thus missing Perbargus ("buzzard cove"?) Beach and Point. Soon you are back among the Japanese knotweed and on the path by which you originally left Portholland. If you use the road to get back to East Portholland, notice how the limekilns were sited in such a way that the limestone could easily be loaded from above.

7 From the car park at East Portholland walk up past the row of cottages on the seaward side of the post office, each protected from stormy seas with double doors, **and follow the acorn sign to the left, beside the sea wall. At the next sign, continue straight on, signposted to St Michael Caerhays, up the side of the valley.** As you go, you will have plenty of time to admire the views of village and coast, and to reflect how much longer one-third of a mile is than it sounds! Don't be surprised if pheasants rise with a squawk and a clatter of wings from the hedges and fields: you are skirting the Caerhays estate. **Cross the stile on your right, then walk with the hedge on your left until passing through the gap in it. Go through the five-bar gate, and then head for the telegraph pole; when a bungalow comes into view aim just to the right of it. Here there are two stiles,** the first made rather awkward to cross by barbed wire, even though the barbs were wrapped in blue plastic.

8 **At the road, turn right for Caerhays Castle and Porthluney Cove; but to visit St Michael Caerhays Church turn left.** On the way you will pass the gatehouse to the castle, and later a commemorative oak tree, dating (like me) from 1937 but still no great size (unlike me). Having recently read Anne Treneer's description of the gardens of Caerhays village in *School House in the Wind,* I was surprised at the rather bleak place we found. The disused school, set back behind ugly walls, was "To Let" when we last walked here. Presumably all the buildings still belong to the Squire, and I suppose their rather drab and stark uniformity reflects the taste of his forebears. (Could they really have admired those brick porches?) The unpretentious little church is all the more charming by contrast, and the members of the tiny congregation who were emerging from mattins gave us a friendly welcome. They assured us that the rusty bracket over the church door was not a relic of a netball court but once supported an oil lamp.

It is worth walking round to the north side of the church for the view of the Caerhays estate, and also to see the very old doorway, now blocked up, with a carving of the Lamb above it. The church guide refers to this as "Pre-Norman". Inside, very little of the ancient workmanship survived what Betjeman calls the "vile" restoration (1864), but there are still some old stained glass and memorial tablets to the Trevanion family of Caerhays, plus a life-size statue of Captain George Byron Bettesworth (1785-1808), who was a member of that family. The Trevanions were, as you may have guessed, related to Lord Byron.

Return the same way. The large farm on your right as you start the descent to the cove is Caerhays Barton, another unappealing group of buildings, dominated by concrete and "galvanise". **If you do not want to go right down to the beach and castle** (and they are both on the route of Walk 4), **you could go through the wooden gate at the far end of the parking-space on the right; if you go right from there on the upper path, you soon join the coastal footpath, avoiding a steepish climb in the process.** For Caerhays, see Walk 4.

9 **From Porthluney Cove, return up the road, and where it bends right go up the steps ahead, signposted to East Portholland.** The coast path runs by the cliff edge at first, passing quite close to Watchouse Point, overlooking Porthluney - presumably another indication of the efforts made by the preventives to cope with smuggling. **Before long, at a field corner the coast path turns a little way inland: you have to walk up to a gate, and this is the link with the path starting at the small car park, as mentioned earlier.** From here on, all is straightforward and easy walking.

WALK 4
CAERHAYS, GORRAN AND DODMAN POINT

Nearly eight miles.
Several shorter versions are possible.

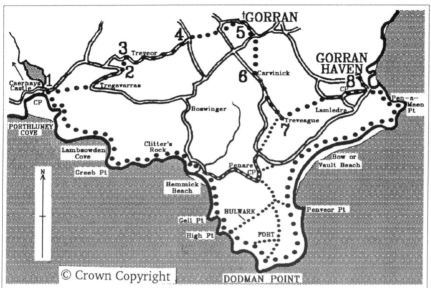

© Crown Copyright

This is definitely a walk to occupy a full day unless you are experienced in coping with the ups-and-downs of the coast path - although in fact the coastal walking between Gorran Haven and Dodman Point is fairly level. The full walk offers a splendid variety of inland and coastal scenery, along with a unique country house set in beautifully landscaped grounds, plus two attractive old villages, perhaps the most impressive prehistoric rampart in Cornwall, and several good bathing beaches. Like Nare Head (Walk 2), Dodman Point offers a great number of attractive "round walks", some of which could include Gorran Churchtown, Gorran Haven or Caerhays, and if you prefer one of these instead of the full route, I suggest you use the Penare car park. There are pubs and shops at Gorran Churchtown and Gorran Haven.

Directions are given from Porthluney Cove (Caerhays Castle), which might be the best point to start the full walk, because it would enable you to get refreshments almost half-way along the route at Gorran Haven. For a medium-length walk omitting Caerhays you could park at Gorran Haven, reading the directions from point 8, and return via Penare and Treveague (see points 6 and 7); and for a walk round the Dodman alone use the National Trust car park at the beautiful old farm of Penare (grid reference SW 999 404). Footpaths to Vault Beach and to Dodman Point are signposted from Penare. All these places are best approached by car from the road south from St Austell to Gorran Haven: consult your map!

27

CAERHAYS CASTLE

It was designed by John Nash, the architect of Buckingham Palace, and replaced a 16th-century mansion which was demolished in 1808. The cost of building it and landscaping the grounds helped to bring ruin on the Trevanion family; their love of gambling also contributed. To quote from Christine Hawkridge's *A History of Gorran,* "The last Trevanion left the ancestral home stealthily by the back door while the bailiffs were approaching the front. The castle remained empty for many years and was robbed of all its movable furnishings. The papier-mâché roofs recommended by Mr Nash were not adequate to cope with Cornish rain, and the roof collapsed, the rain came in, and a family of ducks were observed to be swimming happily in a large puddle on the drawing-room floor." The Williams family (the mining millionaires of Scorrier House: see *The Landfall Book of the Poldice Valley* and the second volume of *Exploring Cornwall's Tramway Trails),* who have owned it since 1852, have restored its original Gothick splendour, and thanks largely to the plant-hunting expeditions sponsored by John Charles Williams (1861-1939) its garden is now known throughout Britain, if not further afield, especially for its rhododendrons and other oriental plants. The grounds cover about sixty acres. Usually the gardens are opened to the public two or three times a year: see the current *Gardens of Cornwall Open Guide.*

1 Close to the gatehouse to Caerhays Castle, cross the little bridge, go through the kissing gate and follow the sign pointing to Tregavarras. Walk just to the right of the clump of trees, mainly holm oaks. From here you get a fine view back over the lake and Porthluney Cove, named from the River Luney, which rises near Ventonwyn Mine, west of Sticker. "Luney" probably means "smooth, even". **The path continues up over the field to a stile on the right of a farm gate near the top-right corner.** (If the field contains beautiful but fearsome-looking Highland cattle with long horns, don't panic: they seem to be always very placid.) **Turn left on the road.**

Porthluney Cove and Caerhays Castle as seen at the start of this walk

2 **Where the road bends left, go straight on, marked Footpath to Treveor, past a row of cottages.** **After the stile, keep by the hedge on the left at first, then cross stepping stones over a boggy patch to another stile and a footbridge.** (Watch your steps here: the planks are getting old, and plant growth may hide the gaps between them.) **Now go up over the ridge to a stile at the top corner,** where there's another fine view.

3 **Turn right on the road and continue past Treveor,** with its lakes on the right. "Treveor" means "big farm", a name that suits it better than "Penveor" suits the rather small headland north of the Dodman; but Treveor is now less of a farm and more of a campsite.

4 **At the T-junction turn left then immediately right over a stile, signed to Gorran.** (The road you have just crossed, Almshouse Hill, takes its name from the parish poor house which used to stand beside it, erected on what James Whetter believes to have been once the site of a *plen an gwary*, a medieval open-air amphitheatre.) **Head slightly left of the church to a stile, cross the road to the next stile, then a third and fourth; at the road in Gorran Churchtown turn right, past (or to!) the pub.** See Walk 5 for a note about the church and village.

5 When you are ready to continue, **go on along the main road, and after a few yards use the new footpath up on the right,** presumably intended mainly for use by the village schoolchildren. **At the road continue straight on through Menagwins ("windy hill") Farm, following the sign to Carvinick. Cross the stile on the left of the farm gate. Now the path goes diagonally to the right, across the field.** Look right to see the modern school buildings which replaced those described by Anne Treneer, burnt down in 1967. **After two more stiles head towards the farm buildings of Carvinick** ("stony camp" - compare The Winnick at Pentewan). **Here it's best to go through the first gate into the farmyard, because the mud around the second one can be spectacular. Go to the road on the right.**

6 **Turn left on the road, and where it bends right go straight on towards Treveague Farm,** whose outbuildings have been converted to holiday accommodation. This farm was advertised for sale in *The West Briton* in 1814, described as "very advantageous for manure, being a quarter of a mile from Gorran-Haven, where lime, sand, ore-weed, caff-fish, and old salt, may be had in the greatest abundance." Caff-fish were pilchards unfit for sale, and the "old salt" had been used for curing fish.

To return to Caerhays without walking to Gorran Haven and possibly cutting out the Dodman too, take the signed path to Penare, through a gate on the right just before Treveague. The path goes across the field through another gate with a footpath sign, then straight on via two more gates to a road. Still continue straight on. From Penare you could join the coast path above Vault Beach, at Penveor Point, at the Dodman, near High Point or at Hemmick Beach: see the map. For Hemmick continue down the road past the NT car park.

7 For the full walk, turn left past Treveague House and go through the metal farm gate (footpath sign: Gorran Haven). The path takes you down an attractive valley. Cross the stream by the stepping stones, go down through the gate, bear left on the gravelled drive, and at the road turn right to go down into Gorran Haven. See the note about this in Walk 5. (If you want the pub - the Llawnroc Inn - go down to the beach, turn left up Church Street and left again up Chute Lane.)

8 From the pub, return to the harbour and turn left at Foxhole Lane. The coast path starts up some steps, signposted to Vault Beach. From here on, few directions are needed; I'll just mention some points of interest, a few possible complications in the route, and some alternative routes that would shorten the walk. As you approach the first headland (Pen-a-maen, "stone head"), either continue around the edge or take the high path. The latter involves some scrambling, both up and down, but rewards you with a good view, and there is also an interesting memorial tablet set in the rock. The large house you soon see up on the right is Lamledra; a road runs from this parallel with the coast path, and this road is closest when you get near to the end of the long beach (called Bow Beach for an obvious reason, or Vault Beach for no reason I know, though it is popularly supposed to be a gloomy link with the "Dead Man" or Dodman), so if you wish you could go up to the road and continue via Penare back to the coast at Hemmick Beach. After about a quarter of a mile, near Penveor ("great head") Point, another track goes off, sharp right, signposted Penare; this track follows the line of the prehistoric bulwark that once defended the fort on Dodman Point. At the point itself, go up to the cross to get the best view seawards. This is the highest point on the south coast of Cornwall, almost 400 feet. It's also worth going a little way inland to see the little watch house, dating from 1795. Back on the coast path, the big wall on the right by the next stile marks the other end of the ancient bulwark.

DODMAN POINT

Just before I came to live in Cornwall, a pleasure boat called the "Darlwin" sank off Dodman Point, drowning all her 31 passengers. At that time I had never seen the Dodman, but my mental picture was of a grim, death-ridden place, and even now when I see its forbidding black bulk in silhouette, with Parson Martin's cross like a churchyard headstone perched on its summit, I can't altogether shake off those associations. It comes as no surprise to learn that in 1699 its name was written as "Deadman Point". The 1994 Gorran Parish Council centenary booklet refers to "the Deadman (never Dodman to locals)". As so often, Anne Treneer puts it best: "Dodman absorbs the blackness of winter ... We called the Dodman, Deadman. Deadman and Vault; the names were permanent reminders of shipwreck and distress though we used them lightly and thoughtlessly enough. Yet something in Dodman subdued us. We never played there."

And yet, of course, it's a place of great beauty with a power to uplift: friends of ours who live nearby say a walk on Dodman Point is the best cure for depression they know. In reality the name has nothing to do with death: Oliver Padel says it derives from the surname Dudman, and Craig Weatherhill with equal confidence states, "The name Dodman is derived from the Cornish word *tomen,* a bank or dyke." One of the most impressive features of the headland is the great Iron Age rampart, up to twenty feet high, which with an outer ditch and another lower bank runs for nearly 2,000 feet across the neck of the promontory. Within the area of nearly fifty acres thus enclosed there must have been quite a large settlement, but so far there has been no excavation to reveal the remains of dwellings; two burial mounds of an even earlier date than the Bulwark are visible, though, and so are parts of a medieval strip field system. For details about that, the watch house and the Dodman Cross, see the National Trust's *Coast of Cornwall* leaflet No. 20.

A lady my wife and I met shortly before *Around Mevagissey* was published painted a vivid picture of the saintly Rector of Caerhays who had the cross set up, George Martin. Anne Treneer knew him for a short time just before "he left the secluded beauty of Caerhays to live, not as a Priest, but as a day-labourer in a London slum. He was one who took literally Christ's warning to the rich young ruler, Sell all that thou hast and give to the poor."

The tranquillity of the Dodman is occasionally disturbed nowadays as a result of the establishment of a Royal Navy gunnery range out at sea between the Point and Polruan, a replacement for the one which used to be near Portland in Dorset. This move has greatly angered many local people, and has been vigorously opposed by the National Trust, which has refused permission for the siting of an observation post on the headland.

Next comes perhaps the toughest stretch on the walk, between High Point and Gell Point - although the path round Lambsowden Cove rivals it. After Hemmick Beach, which is described so lovingly in Anne Treneer's *School House in the Wind,* you pass Clitter's Rock - a quartzite outcrop rather similar to Carn Rocks, north of Gorran Haven - on the hill above you. The path down to Lambsowden Cove is overshadowed by an impressive row of fang-like rocks. In October the cliffs ahead were covered with bracken, brilliant rust-red. The footbridge is followed by a stiff climb; you cross a couple of unusual bridge-like stiles over hedges, and then you are round to Porthluney and a fine view of the castle. The path follows the cliff edge and joins the road where you left it earlier, just to the right of the bridge.

WALK 5
GORRAN AND MEVAGISSEY
Nearly seven miles, with a possible extension of about a mile

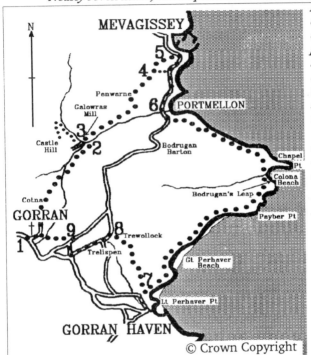

© Crown Copyright

Here is yet another delightful piece of coastline, and it's probably the least strenuous to walk along of any covered in this book. I hardly need to spell out the pleasures of visiting Mevagissey and Gorran Haven; in any case, they are both included in other walks, and the main route of this one reaches only the edges of them. Almost equally enjoyable to walk through are the smaller communities of Portmellon and Gorran Churchtown. Between the latter and Mevagissey is some of the loveliest inland scenery in the region: deep, wooded, lush valleys crowned by an ancient hill fort or settlement which can be visited on a short diversion. Despite the hills, there is again nothing particularly strenuous to cope with, but mud is likely, especially around Galowras Mill. If a pub that serves palatable food is essential for a good walk, you are spoilt for choice on this one, since all four villages have at least one; and all except Portmellon also have shops that sell provisions.

The directions are given from Gorran Churchtown. Although there is no car park there, roadside parking is usually available, and by starting there you give yourself the option of not walking down into Mevagissey or Gorran Haven. This would be a particular advantage at Mevagissey, because it would enable you to reduce the amount of walking along a road which in summer can be busy. It would also avoid parking charges and reduce the risk of getting snarled up in traffic jams. To drive to Gorran from St Austell, take the B3273 south, avoiding Mevagissey by turning right about a mile north of it. Road signs should guide you safely the rest of the way, but a good map would be an advantage. From the Truro direction you could drive to it via Tregony or Grampound and Polmassick, but in either case I would regard the map as essential!

32

GORRAN CHURCHTOWN

The spelling "Gurran", used by William Wynne in his account of his travels in 1755, reflects the way the name is still often said locally, and is faithful to the earliest recorded spelling of the saint's name, "Guron". He moved here after setting up a religious community at Bodmin.

Inside the large, rather empty-feeling church, perhaps the main points of interest are the collection of fifty-three 16th-century bench ends and the brass known as The Lady of Brannell. The list of vicars, near the main entrance, is also worth inspection, since it includes much more historical information than usual. In 1300 (or 1306), for example, the church was "under interdict" because the friends of a Tregony man slew his murderer in the church; in 1473 the vicar, Thomas Marbury, resigned "on account of defect of unsuitability of vulgar tongue (Cornish)"; in 1615 the vicar was "ousted for Royalist tendencies"; in 1735 the parish had 170 families, and in 1790, 400. Originally there was a spire, which was tall enough to be a navigational aid to seamen; it is shown on the back of the fine old carved chair at the east end. The spire was replaced by the present imposing tower early in the 17th century.

The village seems to have changed little since last century, to judge by the old photographs. There is probably no better way to capture the flavour of life there some ninety to a hundred years ago than to read Anne Treneer's *School House in the Wind* (1944, reprinted 1983), a title which reflects the fact that the village is some 300 feet above sea-level. One change that has occurred, though, is that the school she describes was burnt down in 1967 and rebuilt two years later.

1 **From the Barleysheaf Inn at Gorran Churchtown (*) go past the main entrance to the church and turn left. After passing a few cottages take the left turn, following the sign Public Footpath - Galowras Mill. Just before the lane reaches Cotna House, cross the stile on the right, opposite a footpath sign.**

Christine Hawkridge's excellent little *History of Gorran* mentions that the medieval version of "Cotna" was "Crukoner", referring to a barrow: compare "Cruggan" on Walk 5. "In 1854," she adds, "when workmen were planting the gardens of the house being built there for Mr Kendall, they discovered earthen jars filled with the charred remains of human bones." She also mentions a nearby field known as "The Plains", which the eminent Cornish historian Charles Henderson suggested might indicate the former site of Gorran's playing-place or "plain-an-gwarry"; recently, however, Dr James Whetter has found convincing evidence that it was located further west, between Gorran and Treveor.

Cross the field to the stile in the centre of the hedge opposite, then bear slightly left to another stile, and after that go straight on or slightly right across the ridge to a fourth stile on

the right of a gate. **Now the path goes quite steeply down into this beautiful valley, keeping by the fence on the right. After crossing the stile in this fence, don't go down to the valley bottom** (where, incidentally, there used to be a watermill known as Sentries Mill, apparently a corruption of "Sanctuaries": the mill stood on a piece of glebe land). **Follow the footpath sign to the right, through a gate or open gap, and continue ahead beside four oak trees to a wooden stile. Next comes a path through pretty woodland.** This is West Bodrugan Wood Nature Reserve; a notice on the gate at the far end requests walkers to keep to the path, walk quietly and keep dogs on leads. The pool which you pass at the start of the woodland was thickly coated with waterweed in October 1991 - "Ginny Greenteeth" was my wife's name for it, learnt from her father, a Lancashire man.

2 Immediately beyond the five-bar gate turn sharp left and cross the bridge to Galowras Mill, which was the manor mill of Galowras ("Gloeret" in the Domesday Book), about half a mile to the north. The lord of the manor's tenants would have been required to grind their corn at his mill, and in 1795 this mill had two pairs of stones for the tenants' use. The name means "clear watercourse" or "bright ford". Incidentally, when we walked here in 1988 a notice proclaimed that its owner was a Mr Grist.

You might care to make a short diversion here (less than a mile) through attractive countryside to the site of a prehistoric hilltop "castle" with fine views. If so, turn left up the narrow road beside the mill, and almost immediately turn sharp right, through a five-bar gate with a footpath sign attached. Ignore side paths, keeping at first to the grassy (in places muddy and/or cowpatted, I'm afraid) track. The old millstream or "leat", though dry now, is still clearly visible on the right side of the track. After another five-bar gate walk beside the hedge on your left. Here in October the grass was lush, and the woods in the valleys were thick and dark: a delightful scene, completed by the mill house, artistically placed at the focal point of several gentle curves. The path eventually goes down to a small stream which has created quite a large patch of mud. After negotiating that, bear left, joining a track; go through the metal gate, then turn left and go through another, back over the stream. Now the route runs gently uphill towards the hilltop trees. Go through the gap in the hedge (where there was a single strand of barbed wire to cross), then follow the clear uphill path. Soon the sea and the valley down to Portmellon come into view. At about this point the right of way appears to come to an end, rather frustratingly a few yards short of the hilltop, crowned by a valiant little stunted oak. From there the view is even better, including Gorran church. It is a typical site for an Iron Age hill fort, but it seems to have been a civilian settlement, despite the name, "Castle Hill". Return to the mill by the same route.

3 To continue the walk, follow the footpath sign (on the right of Galowras Mill when you first approached it), through a gate and over a footbridge: another spot that's likely to be muddy. Continue round to the right. Now the path runs down the wide valley which reaches the coast at Portmellon. Keep a few yards left of the wooded area around the stream, and then go a little further left to pass through the gap in the hedge ahead. From

there the path is clear. After the next hedge, keep to the main (lowest) path, curving left behind Portmellon to Penwarne (*), a beautiful old farm with particularly impressive outbuildings. **Go through the five-bar gate and walk around the left side and front of the farmhouse to join the main drive, which brings you to a road.**

PENWARNE

The name reflects the house's sheltered position: "end of the alder-marsh". From early times it belonged to the family of the same name, but during the Tudor period it passed through marriage successively to the Coswarths, the Hills and then to John Carew, second son of Richard Carew of Antony, author of the famous *Survey of Cornwall.* I'll let Polsue tell the story: "In 1601, at the siege of Ostend, this John Carew lost his right hand by a cannon ball, on which occasion he evinced considerable fortitude. Returning to his lodgings he threw the amputated hand on the table remarking to the hostess, - "this is the hand that cut the pudding to-day;" he was afterwards called *the one handed Carew.* The loss of his hand was partially supplied by a piece of mechanism curiously contrived and rendered elastic by strings; this artificial hand and his portrait were long preserved at Heligan." (Lake's *Parochial History)* (For Heligan see Walk 6.) John had only one son but many daughters, one of whom was carried off by Turkish pirates. The son left no heir; Penwarne was sold to the Fortescues, and by the time Polsue was writing most of the estate belonged to the Williams family of Caerhays. The house and outbuildings clearly retain much that is old; like The Terrace at Pentewan (Walk 7), Penwarne is said to include stone from the deserted mansion of Polrudden. An advert printed in *The West Briton* when Penwarne was offered for sale in 1812 included this: "The above premises are most admirably situated for manure, being within half-a-mile from Mevagissey, where town-dung may be procured in any quantity, at the low price of one shilling per butt-load, and within a quarter of a mile of Porthmellin, whence sea-sand may be brought at a trifling expense."

4 Turn left on that, and where the road bends right take the footpath almost straight ahead. *(This is the way to go if you want to include Mevagissey in the walk; and even if you don't it might still be worth it for the wonderful view over the harbour and village that it gives you. But if you would prefer to shorten the walk slightly and cut out some road walking, take the path on the right instead. This is shown on the map.)* **As you approach Church Park Farm, notice the old well on the left. Go through the farm gate to the left of the house and turn right, walking downhill with the hedge on your right. After the kissing gate, go right for a few yards, past the entrance to Polhaun. Now the path goes down to the left between concrete-block walls, and you emerge on to the road above Mevagissey harbour.** The temptation to walk down there will be hard to resist, especially if you're hungry and thirsty ... but bear in mind the steep hill back, and that there's a pub at Portmellon too!

5 For the coastal walk south, turn right along the road. Please walk with great care here, since it tends to be busy and there's little in the way of pavements. As you start to descend to Portmellon, notice the road sign, "Beware of Waves".

PORTMELLON

The name could mean "yellow cove", but "mill cove" is more likely. There doesn't seem to be any sign of a mill there now; the fish cellars have gone, too, and so has the famous Mitchell's Boatyard (established 1925, closed 1979), though a board beside the block of six new houses on its site acts as a reminder of it. The launching slip remains, erected in 1941 and largely rebuilt with the addition of rails in 1960, and there's an old, uprooted winch, but both look sadly redundant. The book to read about all this, if you can find a copy, is Percy Mitchell's *A Boatbuilder's Story* (1968).

The pictures on pages 24-7 of Joy Wilson's *Around St Austell Bay* (Bossiney Books, 1986) tell much about Portmellon during last century and the early years of this: they recall the cholera outbreak of 1849, when 115 Mevagissey people died in five weeks and most of the surviving population occupied ordnance tents, each able to shelter 500 people, at Portmellon; they show the many fish cellars, the largest of which occupied part of what is now beach as well as the site of the blue-shuttered houses; and one is of an early car on the beach before the road was built (about 1918). The crossing is a good deal easier nowadays, except in an easterly gale, when you do indeed have to "beware of waves".

6 If you managed to brave the waves and have emerged unscathed, **follow the acorn sign pointing left as you begin to climb the hill on the far side of Portmellon. The first half-mile-or-so of the coast path here is along a made-up drive. Don't be so distracted by the glorious coastal views that you miss another acorn sign directing you to the left.** Somewhere along this stretch of cliffs east of Portmellon a short-lived ochre mine called Wheal Boger was opened in 1836; for more on this topic see the next page. **The clifftop path soon descends towards Chapel Point.**

CHAPEL POINT

This headland was, says Sheila Bird, "capped by an ancient fort", but that is no more evident now than the medieval "lighthouse" chapel that is thought to have stood here. The chapel is sometimes said to be the one from a window of which Tristan jumped when fleeing from King Mark, foreshadowing Bodrugan's later exploit nearby. (See Joy Wilson's *Cornwall, Land of Legend,* Bossiney Books. She believes that some ruined foundation walls in the garden of the middle house are a relic of the chapel.) A different reason for the name of the point is suggested by the Mevagissey Museum's leaflet: the Mevagissey Independents (later the United Reformed Church), founded in 1626, used to hold their meetings on the headland, "where they had good warning of the approach of the authorities." The harmonious group of buildings which now occupy the site were built, largely from stones collected on Colona Beach, in the late 1930s by the architect John Campbell. His friend Frank Baker in *The Call of Cornwall* calls the three white houses "masterpieces", only part of "the celestial city that he had planned at Chapel Point - a city doomed by inane bureaucracy to live only in his imagination". "In face of all the monstrosities of domestic "architecture" which were and are blots on Cornwall's magnificent coast," declares Mr Baker, "Campbell's great work demonstrates the right way to set about it." The National Trust, choosing its adjective with great care, calls the houses "distinctive".

The path then passes above Colona Beach before climbing again, past the National Trust sign, Bodrugan's Leap.

BODRUGAN'S LEAP

Bodrugan Barton, on the site of the Domesday manor of Bodeworgoin, is a little way inland here, still an impressive farmstead but retaining only a few bits of masonry from the great medieval manor house occupied by the family of the same name, whose history has recently been traced by Dr James Whetter in what Philip Payton calls "an astonishingly painstaking study" (*The Bodrugans, A Study of a Cornish Medieval Knightly Family,* 1995). In 1487 Henry Bodrugan, who had supported Richard III, fled, pursued by Lord Edgcumbe of Cotehele; the Edgcumbes were rewarded for their loyalty to the Lancastrian and Tudor cause by acquiring most of the Bodrugan estates. Bodrugan is supposed to have ridden his horse over the cliff. One version of the legend is that he was then taken overseas by a waiting boat, and Dr Whetter believes it is "likely" that the boat was manned by men from Portheast (Gorran Haven). Charles Causley's poem,

"Young Edgcumbe", offers another ending:

And from the height, Bodrugan	And ever did the ocean
Sprang down into the swell	Under Bodrugan's Leap
That tide on tide at the cliff-side	With loving care the body fair
Hammers a passing-bell.	Of Lord Bodrugan keep.

Again, don't miss the acorn sign nearby which directs you to the left side of the wire fence, which for some distance ahead now will oblige you to keep quite close to the cliff edge.

(Some walkers may find this rather unnerving, especially round Payber Point and along the high cliffs beyond. If you would rather not risk it, you could try the inland path from above Colona Beach, which passes through Bodrugan Barton, then turn left on the road to Gorran Churchtown. I have not walked this myself; if it proves impracticable, return to Portmellon by the coast path and take the road from there back to Gorran.)

About half a mile past Payber Point are the whitish, lichen-covered quartzite Carn Rocks (literally "rockpile rocks"); the path keeps to the right of them, but there's a nice little picnic or coffee-break spot on the seaward side of the first rock. From here the view to the right over the houses of Gorran Haven allows you a glimpse of the top of Dodman Point; the nearer headland beyond the village is called Pen-a-maen ("stone head"). The attractive beach you walk above next is called Great Perhaver, which Dr Whetter thinks may mean "Harbour Cove": he speculates that "in early times" this and Little Perhaver (further south) may have been a more suitable place for Gorran harbour than the present site. In 1804 an ochre mine was opened above Great Perhaver beach; at that time the ochre clay was probably quarried, but when the site was re-worked in 1897 by a German company a 40-foot shaft was sunk. An iron landing stage was built down on the beach: see photo 12 in Dr Whetter's *History of Gorran Haven,* Part 2. Dr Whetter says the ruins survive of an engine house at the point where loads of clay were lowered to the landing stage. From there a small tender took the clay out to a larger vessel in deeper water. (Local seiners were afraid that shoals of fish would be scared off by the noisy operation, and when the mining company broke its promise to cease work on the sighting of such a shoal the seiners took revenge by capsizing the tender. This story, and its amusing sequel at St Austell Magistrates' Court, is told in the Gorran Parish Council's centenary booklet, 1994.) The ochre was wanted for burnishing gold and silver, and especially for dyes and paints, but the mine closed when it was found that the clay from deeper levels yielded ochre of poor quality.

The path soon descends to the bungaloid edge of Gorran Haven.

GORRAN HAVEN

From at least medieval times till the 18th century, Gorran was a much more important maritime community than Mevagissey (for example, in the late 16th century 68 Gorran men were listed as sailors, compared with 8 in Mevagissey). Nowadays, Mevagissey still has several working boats, whereas Gorran's fishing fleet consists of "Buccaneer", which takes visitors out fishing in summer. And yet Gorran - once you get down below the retirement villas and the car park - retains much more of the atmosphere of an old fishing and boat-building village, probably because it lacks the obvious picturesqueness of its old rival. (That rivalry sometimes flared into bitter enmity between the fishermen of Gorran and Mevagissey, as the press reported in July 1873: see *Life in Cornwall in the Late Nineteenth Century*, Bradford Barton 1972.)

"Portheast" is Gorran Haven's old name, a corruption of "Porth Just": its little chapel of ease is dedicated to St Just, the same Celtic saint from whom St Just-in-Roseland and St Just-in-Penwith are named. This fascinating little building dates from the 15th century; the Chantry Act (1545-7) caused it to be deconsecrated, and then, in the words of a letter dated 1651, "the fishermen made itt a house to keep their sea tackell therein." Only in Victorian times was it fully restored and returned to use as a place of worship.

Gorran Haven.
The little church is just right of centre.

A pier was built in medieval times, and Dr Whetter claims that by 1270 Gorran had "one of the largest fisheries in Cornwall". It continued to thrive, and in 1720 there were over twenty fish cellars. The harbour was improved in 1820, and in 1888 the Williams family of Caerhays had a new quay built. By then Gorran had thirty boats and sixty fishermen and was famous for boat building and crab-pot making. The limekiln building which so dominates the old village probably dates from 1812. The kilns went out of use for lime burning about 1910 and became a coal store; during the 1930s they were filled in and the top of the building became a car park. The boat pound down on the harbour beach occupies the site of "the big cellar"; next to that was a smaller fish cellar which was converted into a watch house for the preventive officers; and on the other side of the limekilns was the Ship Inn, now the Mermaid café. Photograph No. 21 in Dr Whetter's first volume gives a clear impression of this scene in 1885.

I recommend his work if you want all the details, including lots of references to particular people. Part of the flavour of the good old days is vividly evoked in his accounts of the Gorran men who during lean periods would walk to Newquay and Falmouth in search of work, and of "poor Mrs Kerkin" : "She lived in a terrible way and Henry Johns recalls ... seeing fleas coming out of her clothes by the neck and going back down again." For an easier read, more clearly printed, and a study which puts the salient facts into the context of the parish as a whole, go for Christine Hawkridge's *A History of Gorran,* if it can still be had; and for a lively, well-written "personal portrait" of the village try *Laughs and Sweet Memories* by Archie Smith (Camomile Press, 1992). *The Cornwall Village Book,* produced by the W.I. in 1991, has some interesting "snippets", such as the fact that Rattle Street is so called because it used to be cobbled, and that the name of the owner of the general-store-cum-bakery is Cakebread.

7 The village is well worth a visit, whether or not you want to use the pub or shops; for the pub (actually a hotel called Llawnroc: try reading it backwards) turn right at Chute Lane. But **to complete the round walk without going down into the village, turn right when you reach Cliff Road, following the footpath sign to Trewollock. Now take the first right turning, and at the top of the road turn right where a footpath is marked, between the houses numbered 50 and 53. You cross two stiles, then the path runs along a slight ridge (presumably a grubbed-out hedge) with a wire fence on the right. Keep to the field edge, past a footpath sign at the corner; turn left there, go through the farm gate and walk along the track to Trewollock (or Trewollack) Farm. Keep straight on past the farm buildings, then bear left, through a farm gate to the road.**

8 **Turn left past the front entrance to the farm, and then follow the sign to Gorran.** Soon you pass Trelispen Farm, now run by Dr James Whetter as a "Camping Park" and a Craft Centre. Cream Teas were advertised, but this was October and everything was firmly shut down till next season. Dr Whetter thinks "Trelispen" might mean "farm at the end of the court", though there is no evidence that the Bodrugan manorial courts were held there. **When you reach the main road (Bell Hill), turn sharp right along a minor road marked "Unsuitable for Motors". At the T-junction turn right, and after about a hundred yards cross the stile on the left, where there is a footpath sign to St Goran's Church.**

9 **Now go left, heading roughly towards the church tower. Cross a stile over a wall and continue ahead with the hedge on your right. At the bottom, cross the muddy patch around the stream with the help of a few stepping-stones to a stile with "Footpath" painted on it. Cross that with care: the block on the far side is a bit insecure. Go round by the cottage and at the road turn left for the church, shop and pub.**

WALK 6
MEVAGISSEY, HELIGAN MILL
AND PENTEWAN SANDS
About four miles

This walk begins with one of the most beautiful valleys in the area and ends with a very fine stretch of coast path. Among many other delights, it gives you un-rivalled birds'-eye views of both Pentewan and Mevagissey. In fact, if you have never been to Mevagissey be-fore doing this walk, perhaps you should consider starting the walk at Pentewan, just so that your very first sight of Mevagissey will be from the coast path on the north side - though I must admit that the view from the top of Polkirt Hill, included on Walk 5, is hardly less memorable. Other special attractions include a deserted fishing hamlet - a particularly magical place - and a grand country mansion set among woods. Its garden, once among the most important in Cornwall, has recently been rescued from decades of neglect, and is now one of the county's leading visitor attractions, "The Lost Gardens of Heligan". A short diversion would provide an ideal opportunity to see it.

I mustn't pretend that the walk is an easy one, because there are steep slopes both inland and along the coast. The farm tracks are likely to be muddy, and the woodland paths may sometimes be rather overgrown. There are several rather high stiles to cross, and one gate had to be climbed when we did the walk. About half a mile of the route is along roads which at times carry quite fast traffic. The only pubs or cafés and other "facilities" are in Mevagissey and at Heligan, unless you extend the walk by about half a mile in order to visit Pentewan, which would make a good pausing-place at about the half-way point. If the weather invites bathing, try Polstreath Beach, close to Mevagissey.

Directions are given from the Market Square in Mevagissey (*).

MEVAGISSEY

A village developed here around a church on high ground inland, and another clustered around the nearest sea-cove. The distinctness of their identities in early times is illustrated by the fact that they had different names: the churchtown and parish were "Lammorek" ("church by the sea"?) in the 13th century - later "Levorrick" - and the harbour community was Porthilly ("brine cove"?). An alternative name for the churchtown by about 1400 was a combination of the names of the two saints to whom the church was dedicated, "Memai and Iti", later called "Meva et Ida" or "Meva and Issey"; *hag,* the Cornish word for "and", explains the g in "Mevagissey". It was Porthilly, though, rather than the churchtown, that grew and prospered as a boat-building and fishing community.

The basis of what is now the inner harbour was built in 1430, but the great days of Mevagissey as a port came some three centuries later. In the 1770s the outer harbour and many other additions were made, and a visitor in 1824 claimed that "as a fisher town, Mevagizzey ranks before any other in the county" (F.W.L.Stockdale - whose spelling of the name, by the way, shows how most "locals" still say it). Only 18 years later, however, Cyrus Redding wrote, "This was one of the most noted fishing towns in Cornwall, until the visits of the pilchard to its shores became less frequent." "The streets are wretchedly narrow," he added; "and from this cause the fish are obliged to be carried in baskets to the cellars, between two men with poles over their shoulders. Mevagissy contains some good houses, and the interior of the humblest is remarkable for its cleanliness: yet the odour of the fish is not prevented from being perceptible to the stranger. The fishermen are a fine, active and daring race of men, trained to hardship from their boyhood." The personal stories of the descendants of those men and their families in the first few decades of this century have been remembered in amazing detail by Mary Lakeman in *Early Tide;* and the atmosphere of the place in 1937 is captured perhaps even more vividly by Frank Baker in *The Call of Cornwall:* "The shops were real shops; that is to say, ... you could buy the side of a pig at the drapery by the post office (probably kept under a bed upstairs by Mr Farren), vegetables at Mr Rowe's the butcher's, and everything from a pin to a lawnmower at Mr Rowse's the ironmonger's, opposite The Ship. The narrow little streets were still cobbled. Water came from the green pump between Mr Rowse's and The Ship. The flush lavatory was only in the better houses. Early every morning the human load was carried in buckets to chutes tunnelled into the rock-sides above the harbour." Not just the odour of fish was perceptible to the stranger.

Well, he is catered for more than adequately now, and the dedication to the tourist trade of what was once a self-sufficient community provoked sadness in Miss Lakeman and bitter anger in Mr Baker. But fishing and boatbuilding continue, and there's still a great deal of the old Mevagissey to enjoy. In your exploration of the village you can't do better than take with you the Heritage Coast's *Mevagissey Walkabout* and Peter Bray's collection of old photographs, *Around & About Mevagissey.* Two other valuable books, which have appeared since I wrote *Around Mevagissey,* are Sheila Bird's *The Mevagissey Companion* (1993) and *Cornish Harbour* by H.A.Behenna (1995).

1 **Start by walking away from the harbour, along Church Street.
Watch for the blue sign to the church (on the left), and follow it.**
This minor road soon brings you to the south gate of the churchyard.

MEVAGISSEY CHURCH

As you enter the churchyard on the south side, notice at ground level on
your right the three old gravestones made from sea boulders; two of them
are clearly dated. The story behind the unusual tower is that the original
one was demolished in the 17th century and not replaced till Victorian
times. Two pinnacles from the old tower have been used to decorate the
gate-posts at the north entry to the churchyard. The sundial above the main
door dates from 1713 and is said to bear a punning inscription, but we
found it totally illegible. There is undoubtedly, however, a good crop of
puns inside, on the impressive slate monument, dated 1632, mounted on
the wall near the north altar. The Dart family - father, mother, two large
daughters and six small sons - are all depicted, but the ingenious verses
refer to the deaths of only the father and three sons:

> Death shoots sometimes as archers doe,
> One Darte to finde another;
> But now by shooting hath founde fovr,
> And all layd hear together. ....
> The warfar past the Darts must rest;
> This grave shall be the quiver,
> Where they shall rest till with the blest,
> They be revived for ever.

Another memorial worth study is that to Otwell Hill and his wife (1617),
near the main altar. The pillars dividing the two aisles are of Pentewan
stone (see Walk 7) but the central one is a 19th-century replacement; the
original fell, and was for a time used in the Mevagissey clink to hold
prisoners' chains. It is now in the town's museum. There are a few traces of
the original Norman church, and the font is probably Norman or only a
little later in date; otherwise, the older parts of the church are mostly 15th
century. "It was old until J.P. St Aubyn got at it," is John Betjeman's
response to the efforts of that doyen of Victorian restorers of Cornish

churches. Even its picturesque ancient dedication to Saints Meva and Ida has been supplanted by St Peter, but I don't think Mr St Aubyn can be blamed for (or credited with) that.

To continue the walk, go past the "No Entry" signs, along a lane that brings you to the main road.

2 Cross that with care and turn right along a wide path (almost a minor road, in fact: cars use it) which at first runs parallel with the road. Soon you are walking up the delightful valley leading to Heligan. Between the first and second farm gates you are on a rough track, still running up the right side of the valley. The third gate, a smaller, metal one with a slate stile beside it, brings you to a footbridge.

3 Immediately before the bridge the main walk route turns right, following the narrow path up into the woods - but first it's worth going ahead along the main track for a few more yards to look at Heligan Mill. It was here that some members of what Frank Baker calls "our little art colony" lived during the 1940s: see *The Call of Cornwall.* The mill itself is the building on the left just past a comparatively modern cottage. A millstone lies near the water tank; the waterwheel was against the right-hand end wall of the building, and the remains of the leat are on the left side of the main track as it continues uphill.

Heligan Mill as shown on a postcard of about 1900

To visit the garden at Heligan House (*), go on up that track for about a further half mile. Ivor Herring, in an article in "Cornish Garden", 1983, referring to the grounds of Heligan in Victorian and Edwardian times, writes that "a visitor recalled you could walk from Heligan Mill to the house in carpet slippers, the paths being so well kept." At that period, the route may have been through the Japanese Garden in the valley; during the time of the Tremaynes the people of Mevagissey were permitted to walk up through that on Sunday afternoons. In recent years, before the "finding" of the "lost gardens", you might have needed a machete there - and even on the track those carpet slippers would do well to survive the journey.

HELIGAN HOUSE AND GARDEN

Heligan (said, at least by the purists, with the stress on the second syllable) means "willow-tree". The manor came to the Tremayne family in the 16th century. The house they built in 1603 was drastically altered in 1692, given an extra storey plus a wing in 1809-10 and finally another wing in 1830, thus becoming "one of the handsomest and most commodious mansions of the county" (Lake's *Parochial History*). It had a long drive from the Pentewan Valley, passing under the road near Peruppa Farm.

As far back as 1650 the Tremaynes began developing a magnificent 22-acre garden, but it was in 1780 that the design of the current gardens was laid out, when Henry Hawkins Tremayne commissioned Thomas Gray for the purpose. By about 1910 there were walled gardens, peach houses, melon grounds, an Italian Garden, a Japanese Garden, a wishing well, a summer house, a grotto, an area called "Flora's Green" where the ladies of the house are said to have danced, one of Britain's largest and finest sets of bee-boles (recesses in a wall, used to give shelter to straw bee-skeps before movable-frame bee-hives were introduced into Britain in 1862) - and most important of all, a superb collection of plants, many of them introduced by a famous Victorian plant-hunter, Sir Joseph Hooker. The rhododendrons at Heligan were particularly celebrated. From about 1900 the "new garden" was developed, and this attracted a visit by King George V and Queen Mary. (A further royal connection according to local belief is that Heligan was considered as a possible home for the Duke of Windsor and Mrs Simpson.) The Tremaynes have not lived there since World War I, when the house became a hospital; then it was let to a succession of tenants, and now it is divided into some twenty flats. The garden has, for the most part, been allowed to run wild for at least the last fifty years. Frank Baker described in *The Call of Cornwall* (1976), "Decaying woods where sprawling rhododendrons clutch out above the fallen trunks of ash and willow, monstrous fungi, blackberries large as solitaire marbles ..."

In recent years, much work has been done - mainly on the borders nearest the house - by the occupants of one of the flats, Ivor and Maisie Herring, and late in 1990 an ambitious project to restore the whole garden got under way, thanks largely to the energy and enthusiasm of Tim Smit, a former rock-and-roll producer who came from London with the intention of setting up a studio in Cornwall, but instead fell in love with "the lost garden". With the help of a management team, local people and the British Trust for Conservation Volunteers, rapid progress was made. In 1993, 20,000 paying visitors had come to the garden by early August; the total in 1995 was 200,000, making Heligan the most-visited private garden in Britain. Visitors are given a fascinating guided tour lasting about two hours. A point of special interest for me as a keen grower of vegetables and soft fruit is the 2-acre kitchen garden, stocked with varieties in use during Victorian times. Much remains to be done, including the reclamation of a 30-plus-acre valley south-east of the house, not far from section 3 of the walk route.

The Lost Gardens of Heligan are open all year except Christmas Day, from 10am to 6pm (5pm in winter), last admission 90 minutes before the garden closes. There are shops for sale of gifts, guide books and plants, and refreshments are available.

The first part of the woodland path up from the footbridge looks as if it may get overgrown at times. Soon it becomes an attractive sunken path; presumably it was once a farm track or narrow lane down to the mill. One section, where it runs between open fields, is quite steep uphill; then it levels off as it runs along the left edge of more woodland, and here two or three fallen trees necessitated first a small diversion to the right and then a little ducking and crawling. **At the end of the woods, go through the gate and follow the direction shown by the yellow arrow on it, keeping beside the hedge on your right.** Here you have a beautiful view of wooded valleys, with the Georgian Heligan House prominent. **The tractor track brings you to a road via a gate just to the right of an electricity sub-station.**

4 Turn right on the road. PLEASE TAKE CARE ON THIS BUSY ROAD, and walk facing the oncoming traffic. Luckily, you don't **have to stay on it for long: take the minor road on the left, marked "Unsuitable for Heavy Goods Vehicles", and then at the T-junction turn left. This rather wider road is used by some fast traffic, so please again be very careful:** don't be too distracted by the view of Pentewan and Black Head. **Eventually you come down to the main St Austell - Mevagissey road.**

5 *To visit Pentewan, turn left on the main road, and then right.* **To return to Mevagissey, cross the road and take the path on the right at the entrance to the Pentewan Sands Caravan Park.** This occupies an area of low dunes known as The Winnick, which was also an old name for the St Austell River. The Winnick used to be a good place for picnics and games, and it attracted day-trippers such as those on Sunday School outings before World War I, who were brought down by rail from St Austell in cleaned-out china-clay wagons. (See A.L.Rowse's *A Cornish Childhood.*) I believe there are now plans to move the mobile homes further inland and restore the old character of the place. **The path leads up to the main road and then continues as the coast path, still running beside the road for a few hundred yards. Cross the stile on your left, and now the path takes you to the cliffs and quite steeply down to the ruins of Portgiskey.**

When the pilchard fishery in the west of England was at its height, in the 18th and early 19th centuries, a small community dependent on fishing and boatbuilding flourished at Portgiskey. Now only these poignant ruins remain as evidence of the cottages and their gardens, the pilchard cellars, the quay ... Even Port Quin, which according to the legend repeated by all the guide books was abandoned after all the menfolk were drowned in one terrible storm, lacks something of the atmosphere of this place, if only because the National Trust has provided a car park there and made the old cellars and cottages into holiday accommodation. The magic of Portgiskey prompted E.V.Thompson (a local resident nowadays) to use it as a setting in his novels *The Restless Sea* and *Polrudden.*

The coast path now crosses a footbridge and three stiles and takes you on a long, stiff climb to Penare Point. (This is one of three places called Penare or Pennare in the area covered by this book; see the note on Nare Head in Walk 2.) One consolation as you climb is the

Portgiskey

magnificent cliff scenery close at hand (but don't twist your ankle in a badger-hole as you look at it); and at the top you have first a splendid view of Pentewan and the coast to Black Head, and then a delightful one ahead over Mevagissey and Portmellon to Chapel Point. **Next there is a descent towards the attractive Polstreath ("stream-pool"?) Beach; the coast path stays well above it, but still there is another quite stiff climb before you reach a short flight of steps at the edge of Mevagissey. Go straight on across the playing field and down past the Coastguard Station to the harbour.**

To find the Mevagissey Museum, on Island Quay, turn sharp left at the bottom. It is open from Easter to October each year. One of the best village museums I know, it deserves at least a couple of hours of your time. The building itself, dating from 1745, is worth study, retaining as it does many features of the boatbuilder's shop it originally was: the big old lathe is still in the joiner's shop, for example. Among the larger exhibits are an apple crusher, a cider press, a horse-operated barley thresher, and the one which gets most attention from visitors, a complete Cornish kitchen. In addition there is, of course, a huge collection of small items which is constantly being added to. "There is always something new to  see", as the leaflet says; and the people who run the Museum are local-history enthusiasts who will probably be able to answer all the questions about Mevagissey that a small book like this has to ignore.

WALK 7
MEDIUM AND LONG WALKS BASED ON PENTEWAN
Just over three miles or nearly six miles

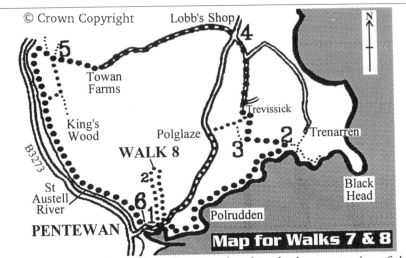

As the large number of boxed notes related to the longer version of this walk implies - and they do little more, to be honest, than scratch the surface - it is one of exceptional historical interest. In terms of scenery, too, it is beautiful and varied, including some fine cliffs, two lovely but very contrasting valleys, woods and high, open farmland. As usual, the coastal section is the most strenuous ("the only cliffs in Cornwall which have absolutely defeated me," declares J.R.A.Hockin in "Walking in Cornwall"- but they're not nearly as bad as they look!). If after walking the coast you'd rather not undertake the full route, the medium-length alternative offers a comparatively easy return to Pentewan, using a road which carries a moderate amount of traffic in summer but compensates for that by being mostly downhill and commanding good views. Roads, apart from extremely minor ones that rarely see more than the occasional tractor, are almost completely avoided on the longer walk. A recommended "extra" would be to explore the woods in the Pentewan Valley, which have quite recently been opened to the public. Pentewan has toilets, shops and a pub, and these are the only such facilities en route; if you plan to start the full-length walk in the morning and have lunch at Pentewan, you could use one of the car parks provided for visitors to the woods, on the left of the B3273 as you drive south from St Austell (grid references: SX 007 497 [just past the concrete products works south of London Apprentice] or 006 487), picking up the directions part-way through point 5. The valley path described in section 2 is likely to be muddy, and in wet spells very muddy indeed; an alternative route through Trenarren is suggested. See also the comments in section 3 about a muddy stream that has to be crossed on the medium-length route.

Directions are given from the small free car park almost opposite the Ship Inn at Pentewan. See the start of Walk 8 regarding buses.

PENTEWAN

Pentewan and the Pentewan Valley are fascinating places to explore, particularly for anyone interested in tin streaming, the china clay industry, ships, harbours and early mineral railways. In the directions and other boxed notes I have given quite a lot of detail, but the history of the area is so rich and complex that I cannot hope to do it justice in the space available. Luckily, several leaflets and small books are easily obtainable locally which will enable you to understand how Pentewan developed and how all the observable details fit into a pattern. For a very brief outline, get *A Short History of Pentewan,* written by K.M. Batchelor for the local Old Cornwall Society. *About Pentewan and Pentewan Valley,* produced by the Pentewan Valley Chamber of Commerce, includes many fascinating snippets about the area generally as well as the particular businesses featured. *Pentewan* by R.E.Evans and G.W. Prettyman (1986) is an interesting and well illustrated 32-page booklet clearly set out in sections; the same two authors produced a good selection of archive photographs entitled *Pictorial Pentewan* in 1994. Best of all for an understanding of the docks and railway is M.J.T.Lewis's *The Pentewan Railway* (Twelveheads Press, 1981); but if you don't have the time or inclination to delve as deeply as Mr Lewis does, do at least take a close look at his plan of Pentewan in 1906 (page 13): this, together with the section on Pentewan Block and Sand Works in *Pentewan,* would go a long way towards enabling you to interpret the details. For a more personal angle, try *Rail and Sail to Pentewan* by John Henry Drew (also Twelveheads, 1986), the recollections of a foot-plateman on the mineral railway whose father was the engine driver from 1887 till 1913. See also Liz Luck's brief but evocative portrait of the village in *South Cornish Harbours.*

One thing I will add which you won't find in any of those is that the sand-bar on Pentewan beach used frequently to make an appearance on television, because it was chosen by Lloyds Bank in October 1989 as the setting for its commercials featuring the black stallion galloping along the shore. In fact, two stallions were filmed, Concara and Beatos (the latter had to have his white "socks" painted out), and two pretty mares were strategically placed in order to spur the males on!

1 Start by walking past the pub, toilets, village square (two other pubs used to be in the square: The Hawkins Arms now transformed to Piskey Cove, and The Jolly Sailor probably now the Post Office Stores), **and the harbour basin, and up Pentewan Hill. Turn right at The Terrace.**

The little Anglican church of All Saints and the delightful houses with their long colonnaded verandah owe their existence, like so much else in Pentewan, to Sir Christopher Hawkins, and date from 1821, but some things here are much older. For example, many of the windows of the houses look Tudor or Jacobean, and it seems probable that they and some of the stone in the walls were taken from the ruins of the old house at Polrudden. Part of the south wall of the church may be even older - possibly Norman - and the remains of arches at the back of the houses lend weight to the belief that this

is the site of a small monastery. An old name for The Terrace was Monks' Walk. The new church, apparently little-used as a place of worship, became a carpenter's workshop for a time, but was re-opened as a church in 1878.

At the far end of the Terrace a sign indicates the coast path. All along the part of it included on this walk you will have a sturdy fence topped with barbed wire to your left, but fortunately this first bit is the only one where you are hemmed in closely on both sides and made to feel like an enemy threatening invasion. Just in case you happen to be slow on the uptake, a notice warns you not to trespass on the cliffs and fields of Polrudden.

POLRUDDEN

Perhaps indeed the fear of invasion does haunt those who live at this farm.

John Polruddon	They saw his wine
All of a sudden	His silver shine
Went out of his house one night,	They heard his fiddlers play.
When a privateer	"Tonight," they said,
Came sailing near	"Out of his bed
Under his window-light ...	Polruddon we'll take away."

Charles Causley's poem goes on to tell how they "bore him down the height"; he never returned, and the great house fell into ruins. The story was first written down by John Norden early in the 17th century. A.L.Rowse in "The Story of Polruddon" *(West-Country Stories)* speculates that John Polruddon (pronounced "Polreddon", says Rowse) acquired his wealth from the highly-valued Pentewan stone quarried on his land, from the Duchy of Cornwall Freestone Quarry. It was used in St Austell, Fowey, Lostwithiel, St Sampson's (Golant), Bodmin, Mevagissey and other churches, as well as mansions such as Trewithen.

Polrudden has a special place in the history of Cornish mining as the site of the first attempt in the county to smelt copper on a commercial scale (1690-7). In view of its remoteness from the main copper-producing areas it's no surprise that the enterprise failed. Copper smelting requires very high temperatures and therefore uses much more coal than tin smelting, so the British copper-smelting industry was based in South Wales.

What looks like a tiny coastguard lookout hut stands on a high point not far from the farm buildings; beyond that, the path curves around Polrudden Cove and climbs to the top of the high cliff on the far side, where the quarries are - not only to the left of the path, but in the cliff-face too. Richard Carew mentions that Pentewan stone was "digged out of the sea cliffs" *(The Survey of Cornwall*, completed by 1602). At low water the remains can be seen of a jetty where the stone was loaded direct on to barges. It looks as if it must have been a risky operation, and indeed in 1830 when J.T.Austen (later called Treffry) was obtaining stone for his new harbour at Par, three of his vessels were wrecked while loading at "Clift Quarry", Polrudden. Soon after the quarry comes a steep descent and an almost equally steep rise: 53 steps to climb. In the distance ahead is Black Head, and just this side of that is Hallane beach. First there is a path down to another small beach, and the coast path drops to a wooden bridge over a dry stream-bed (dry in August, at least); then comes the big climb to the top of the most impressive cliff in these parts, called The Vans (Cornish, *ban,* peak). It's a long haul but not horribly steep, and perhaps you will have strength enough to peer down at the natural arch in the cliffs as you climb, and to notice that Carlyon Bay beach and the church spire at Charlestown are visible across the promontory when you finally reach the top. Daniel Lysons *(MAGNA BRITANNIA,* 1814) refers to "an oval camp, called *The Van",* and indeed this does seem a very likely site for a prehistoric settlement. Now a flight of steps helps you down the steep slope. Soon you are walking through beautiful woodland, and reach a bridge over a stream.

2 Here turn left to continue the walk (unless you want to visit Hallane beach and Trenarren first: strongly recommended. See Walk 9.). Now you are on a narrower path that runs beside the stream up a lovely wooded valley. Here and there the path may be a little overgrown. *(If the valley path is too muddy, you could avoid it by walking up through Trenarren and continuing on the road to Lobb's Shop; there turn left for the direct way back to Pentewan, or for the full walk follow the directions from point 4.)* **There are three gates to go through while you are among the trees, and then you enter an open field. Keep to the bottom of the slope,** passing a tiny pump-house delivering water to the farm above, **till you reach a metal gate.**

3 **Until and unless a more direct path is provided, you now do** *not* **go through the metal gate but climb the steep hill on the right, keeping beside the hedge to your left at first, then continue over the brow of the hill. When Trevissick farm buildings come into view, make for the farm gate to the left of them. Go through that and turn left.**

FOR THE THREE-MILE WALK: go past the open-sided barn and then turn sharp left into a field. Follow the obvious track as it curves downhill, fords a muddy stream, where you are likely to be glad of a pair of wellies unless you are prepared to get wet feet, **and continues uphill to a kissing gate beside the road to Pentewan; turn left on that.** The road, like most others in these parts, is protected most of the way by high banks or hedges, but there are fine views ahead as it begins to slope down towards the village, and near Polrudden farm look right for a glimpse of Glentowan in its little valley, visited on Walk 8.

FOR THE LONGER WALK: follow the cob wall as it turns right. This takes you past Trevissick farmhouse.

The farmhouse is believed to date back to the 13th century, although the front was rebuilt in Queen Anne's time following a fire. A.L.Rowse, who includes a photograph of the house in *St Austell,* refers to the "big Jacobean hall-kitchen at the back". Trevissick farm's land now stretches from just north of the old quarry at Polrudden to Silvermine Point, not far south of Porthpean (more than three miles of the coast path), its western boundary being the road running south from Lobb's Shop towards Pentewan. Once, the farmer told us, this territory was divided among five farms and supported 22 people; now it is just one farm run by four people, and nowadays even those four are hard-pressed to make a decent living out of it.

Go straight on along a minor road, and on joining a slightly wider one still continue ahead.

4 **Next comes the "main" road to Pentewan, Porthpean and St Austell. Cross that and walk past the few houses that make up Lobb's Shop** - presumably once the site of a blacksmith's shop. Not surprisingly, the hamlet seems to have played a part in the activities of smugglers using the nearby small beaches: "We know," writes Mary Waugh, "from the reminiscences of a gardener then (i.e. during the 1830s) employed on the Penrice estate that all sorts of illegal happenings took place at Castle Gotha and Lobb's Shop ... The insatiable demands of the local miners ensured a ready market for the spirits landed at all these beaches." *(Smuggling in Devon and Cornwall,* 1991). This little road - hardly more than a farm lane - runs along a ridge, so the occasional gaps in the roadside banks offer wide views. It is called Towan Road, and it ends at the twin Towan farms, East and West.

TOWAN

If you read the historical notes made by Thomas Tonkin (d. 1742), you may be surprised to find Towan described as "the chief place" in St Austell parish. Towan was the head farm of the Saxon royal manor of Tewington, which appears in the Domesday Book as Dewintone, and was one of the seventeen Cornish manors included in the Duchy of Cornwall when Edward III created the Duchy in 1337. It was therefore an administrative centre with its own manorial court or "leet", and this led William Hals to declare that "Tewington" (or Towington or Tawington) means "*silence in town* or *extraordinary silence in town,* viz. when the court sitteth" - which is fairly typical of early efforts to interpret Cornish names. Tonkin rejected this theory, mentioning the common meaning of *towan* (sand-dune), but preferring "hillock" for this particular place. Oliver Padel in *Cornish Place-Names* adds a further suggestion, that the St Austell River might once have been called the Tewyn, which is similar to the name of a river in Wales, and could mean "bright, shining river". That would make better sense of the name Pentewan as "foot of the Tewyn" rather than "foot of the sandhills". Lake's *Parochial History* mentions a baptismal well at Towan, "over which is an ancient building ... in the early English style of architecture, covered with an arched roof granite." The well is now dry, but its Pentewan stone building was restored by the St Austell Old Cornwall Society in 1937 and has been maintained since then by the farmer at East Towan, on whose land it stands. Known locally as "the wishing well", it is not visible from the public footpath, but you may be able to get directions to it at the farms. It is also known as "the chapel well"; there is no sign of a chapel here now, but some old field names seem to confirm that there was one, and the great student of Cornish saints, Canon Doble, has suggested that both chapel and well may have been dedicated to St Touinianus ... yet another possible explanation of the place names!

Go through the gate ahead, cross West Towan's farmyard, and keep more-or-less straight on along the main track, ignoring the one that branches off to the left. Soon you have a fine view to the right, including St Austell and, further left, the engine house of Great Polgooth mine, perched on its hilltop. **On reaching a metal gate ahead, take the grassy track on the right** - very attractive but liable to be muddy, especially where it begins to slope down more steeply into Peckhill Wood. It looks like an old route, sometimes running in a cutting with mossy banks, and we wondered if it had once been used by packhorses. The owner of East Towan farm told us that in his grandfather's time - 50 or more years back - horses were used to haul timber up it. **Eventually it brings you down to a small parking space where there are gates into the woods**: Shepherdshill to the right, Peckhill and King's to the left. (King's Wood had belonged to the Crown until the execution of Charles I; in about 1650 it was purchased by the Sawle family of Penrice.)

5 Here another choice presents itself: either (A) go down fairly directly to the riverside path, or (B) get to it by means of the winding and probably muddier paths through the woods.
FOR (B): go through the gate or over the stile on the left side of the parking space. Walk along the wide track for about 300 m. and then take the narrow path down on the right (unless, of course, you want to explore the various tracks and paths in King's Wood first). **Now all you need to do is keep heading downhill towards the sounds of traffic on the main St Austell - Pentewan road. Probably the easiest route is to take the slightly narrower path on the left where the main one starts to curve right. After a short scramble down you will reach a small stream (actually a leat, as explained

later). Go left a few yards and cross this by means of the plank (if it's still there!), then turn left and soon you will reach the riverside path/cycleway, just south of a second small parking space. Turn left for Pentewan, and continue reading after the next paragraph.

FOR (A): Continue down the main track (not through either gate). Ignore the first left turning, but just after crossing the small leat mentioned above take the next track on the left, which soon brings you down to the river, where you turn left. After about half a mile on the riverside path/cycleway you will reach a second small car park near a bridge - one of the official entrances to the woods. Still continue beside the river.

You are now walking down the Pentewan Valley. The river is given as the St Austell River on the maps, but old names for it include Clissey, Gover and Winnick or Vinnick (the last two probably meaning "stony"), and until quite recently it was usually known as the White River because of the huge tonnages of china-clay waste that found their way into it as it flowed down from Hensbarrow, discolouring not only the river but also the sea, which only a few years back was commonly milky in appearance well out into St Austell Bay. The river is clear now (all discharges of china-clay residues since 1973 have gone to special mica dams or worked-out pits), although in parts it's often hard to tell, because of the jungle of Japanese knotweed which is rapidly colonising it. This section of the riverside path, running along a small embankment, marks the course of the Pentewan Railway (*), but about a mile north of Pentewan harbour the line curved east, leaving the riverside.

THE PENTEWAN RAILWAY

In several of my earlier books I have written about the first two railways to be built above ground in Cornwall: the Poldice Plateway or Tramway (1809) and the Redruth and Chasewater Railway (1825). Only three years after the latter was built, work started on a single-track line of about 4ft. 6in. gauge designed to enable freight to be carried efficiently between St Austell and the new docks at Pentewan, and by June 1829 horses were drawing wagons along it, although in fact the gentle gradient enabled much of the seaward trip to be accomplished by gravity, as *The West Briton* reported in 1830: "four wagons linked together with about fifteen tons of china clay on them, are put in motion at the depot at St Austell by two men gently impelling them ... Their speed gradually increasing, ... they proceed with the celerity of a mail coach, ... the man who has charge of them having to put his horse to a gallop in order to keep up with them. Having arrived at level ground, ... the conductor attaches his horse to the foremost carriage, and they are thus drawn to Pentewan wharf where a greater quantity of china-clay is shipped for Liverpool, Scotland, &c. than from any other port in England." Locomotives were not introduced until the 1870s, when the gauge of the track was reduced to 2 feet 6 inches. China clay was, from 1873 onwards, loaded into vessels from a low trestle viaduct on the south-west side of the harbour basin; the main freight carried inland was coal, which was loaded into the wagons from the opposite side, near the Ship Inn. The railway played a vital role in the local economy, but its fortunes fluctuated with those of the docks, and the masses of sand deposited by the St Austell River frequently disrupted the operation of the railway by causing the river to flood. The worst disadvantage it suffered from was that it did not reach the china-clay pits it was designed to serve, and road transport (namely, horses and carts) always had to be used to link them to the St Austell terminus. Closure came in 1918, when the Government requisitioned the engines, rolling stock and track as part of the war effort. Some of the buildings at St Austell West bridge terminus may still be seen.

Running down the valley a little east of the river is a leat (millstream), actually the tailrace carrying away the water that once turned the waterwheel at Molingey Mill near London Apprentice. Rather than return the water direct to the river, the long tailrace was cut to provide power at the Wheal Virgin Streamworks, and later it served to fill the four ponds or reservoirs which were dug in order to flush out the harbour.

WHEAL VIRGIN & HAPPY UNION STREAMWORKS

Although the Hensbarrow area, where the St Austell River rises, is best known now as a producer of china clay, it has also been an important source of tin, and for millions of years alluvial tin has been deposited in the Pentewan Valley. As explained in Walk 14, the Polgooth district had some of Cornwall's greatest tin mines, and for several centuries the tin deposits in the valley were enriched by waste washed down from there. William Borlase (1758) called the Pentewan Valley "the most considerable stream of tin in Cornwall." There were several small and ancient streamworks at the St Austell end of the valley, one of which, at Trewhiddle, became famous late in the 18th century when streamers discovered a hoard of Saxon silver. Two larger streamworks operated near Pentewan: one called Happy Union, on the west bank of the river not far above the beach, and the other called Wheal Virgin, about half a mile upriver from there, on the east side. Both were apparently flourishing by 1780, and may have been very much older than that; tin streaming was probably carried out on the Wheal Virgin site as much as 3,000 years ago, to judge by the discovery in 1852 of a shaft considered by archaeologists to date from the Bronze Age. It was lined with oak timbers and hurdles of oak twigs, and the top of the shaft was 3 metres below the 1852 surface. In the previous year the Wheal Virgin streamers had found a beautifully made and well preserved wooden tankard with a bronze handle, and this is thought to have been made in the 1st century AD. It can now be seen in the Royal Cornwall Museum in Truro.

Just in case you imagine tin streaming to have been a variation on panning for gold, I ought to point out that the tankard is thought to have been found nearly 30 ft below the surface; at Happy Union the "tin ground" was even further down, probably as much as 54 ft (14 ft of silt, 20 ft of sea sand and a top layer of 20 ft of river gravel); and to reach those depths all the streamers had was shovels and wheelbarrows. Add to that the labour involved in raising tin-bearing gravel to surface, preparing the ore for smelting, and keeping the workings reasonably dry, and you will see why George Henwood (1860) described streaming as "an avocation ... requiring a hardihood of frame not often found in underground miners."

In fact, of course, tin streaming did sometimes involve underground mining, as for instance in Restronguet Creek, and this evidently applied to Happy Union, which was visited in 1783 by Rudolph Eric Raspe, creator of Baron Munchausen. He wrote that he saw there "a very well organized underground tramroad", and this has been claimed as the first railway to be built in Cornwall. A plan of Wheal Virgin, dated 1861, shows two shafts and a level nearly 70 feet deep.

Happy Union seems to have closed in 1837, but Wheal Virgin continued till about 1874; both made an important contribution to the silting which so plagued Pentewan harbour. The normal practice of the streamers was to back-fill as they dug out new tin-ground; that explains why there are no obvious deep holes left in the large areas they worked.

For a detailed account of tin streaming methods and the discoveries made in the Pentewan Valley, see *Tin in Antiquity* by R.D.Penhallurick.

An unexplained mystery attached to the Happy Union streamworks is the discovery there in about 1829 of the jawbone of a California Great Whale, now on display at the Cornwall Geological Museum in Penzance.

6 The path enters Pentewan opposite a former smithy which later became a cattle-shed and coal store and is now "The Tree House". Turn left. Notice the small sluice-gate on your left, once part of the flushing-out system mentioned above and in the note about the harbour. This sluice was refurbished in 1991-2 by members of the Pentewan Old Cornwall Society, with materials supplied by the owners, Pentewan Sands. Soon you will come to the car park, the Ship Inn and Pentewan Harbour - not, perhaps, one of the most attractive harbours in Cornwall, but it has rightly been called "a fascinating natural museum of industrial Cornwall" (Brenda Duxbury: *About Mevagissey*), and as such it is well worth exploring.

PENTEWAN HARBOUR

Fowey was a natural choice as the southern end of "The Saints' Way" when that footpath was devised (see *Around Padstow* and *Around the River Fowey*), but Pentewan could have been picked instead, because it too was on a prehistoric cross-county trading route. Its cove was therefore an important beaching-point from very early times, and that importance grew with the increasing popularity of Pentewan stone and the boom in the fishing industry. A small harbour was built in 1744.

The mineral wealth of the Pentewan valley, where rich deposits of alluvial tin had been streamed for centuries, and of the high land from which the St Austell River flowed (tin and china clay), convinced Sir Christopher Hawkins of Trewithen (see Walk 18), who owned much land in and around Pentewan as well as china-clay works, that Pentewan needed to be converted into a modern, efficient port. Work started in 1818 and took eight years: the old harbour basin was enlarged and deepened, new quays were built and dock gates and cranes installed.

Two other things that were done are particularly significant. Firstly, a small reservoir was built just north of the basin, fed by the stream flowing down the little Glentowan valley; the hope was that sand and silt collecting in the harbour basin and entrance channel could be flushed out periodically by opening the reservoir's sluice gates. Secondly, a 500-foot-long jetty was built on the south side of the harbour entrance to steer the water of the St Austell River as far away as possible from the harbour.

But neither the reservoir nor the jetty could overcome the problems created by the millions of tons of waste pouring down the river from the stream works and clay pits, and the history of Pentewan harbour is dominated by the ceaseless battle with the sand. In 1831 a 160-foot breakwater was added to the jetty; in 1872 four new reservoirs were built, this time in the main valley, fed by the leat from Molingey Mill, as mentioned in the directions. These and other measures brought at least short-term benefits, and the harbour did have several busy and prosperous periods, but a report in the *West Briton* of 28 February 1862 describes an all-too-common situation: "In Pentewan Creek sixteen small ships have been detained for five weeks to the great loss of their owners and others concerned. These vessels draw from eight to nine-and-a-half feet of water, and they cannot get out in consequence of a sand bank having drifted into the channel ..." No cargo vessel has entered the harbour since 1940, and even then only the entrance channel could be used.

For a much fuller account of the history of the harbour, and information about the industry which grew up from about 1900, selling sand from the beach and using it to make concrete blocks, read *Pentewan,* by R.E.Evans and G.W. Prettyman. The rails which can still be seen near the old quays are relics of that enterprise; so too are most of the unlovely buildings on the south side of the harbour basin, now used as workshops and the local sailing club's headquarters.

Pentewan harbour

WALK 8
A VERY SHORT WALK AT PENTEWAN
About a mile

> *My wife and I did this walk during an exceptionally soggy June, and we were only about a quarter of the way round when the heavens opened. We hastily donned our rainwear, and within five minutes the limitations of its ability to hold the floods at bay had been cruelly exposed ... It must say something about the attractiveness of this little walk that we both remember it with pleasure. Even without the delights of water dripping and splashing from every leaf, I'm confident you will find it an enjoyable way to spend an hour or less of your time at Pentewan. The route is shown on the map for Walk 7.*

Pentewan is south of St Austell: take the B3273 road. There is a fairly frequent "Hoppa" bus service between St Austell and Pentewan. Directions for the walk are given from the car park almost opposite the pub.

1 From the car park, walk past the pub and turn left along Glentowan Road, passing the Village Hall. Go through the gate ahead and up the narrow path on the left, as directed by the Public Footpath sign. Soon you are walking up an attractive valley, with a good view of the sea behind. After about a quarter of a mile you will reach the deserted and semi-derelict buildings of Glentowan. For some discussion of the meaning of the name, see the note on Towan in Walk 7. Glentowan was built as a shooting-lodge for the Sawle family of Penrice, later became a farmhouse, and has now been unoccupied for over forty years.

2 Just past Glentowan you are presented with a choice of three paths. Take the middle one. Go through the gate into woodland. Now the path continues on the right, descending gently at first, then steeply. At the bottom, a few stepping-stones should help you cross a muddy area without too much squelching. Beyond the stile there are more - and better - stepping-stones, and then the path, as it reaches the east side of the valley (known locally as "The Brake") becomes shady, almost tunnel-like; so, at least, it seemed during that June rainstorm. The O.S. map indicates "Quarries (dis)" and an "Adit" in this area. Perhaps these are visible from the path at a time of year when the foliage is less luxuriant. An adit is a shaft designed to drain the water from mine workings; most adits come to the surface on cliff-faces or in valleys like this. What mining took place here I don't know, and it is possible that this adit drained the quarries. There are some comments on the quarries north of Pentewan in the note about Polrudden, Walk 7. Gradually you will emerge into the open as you head south, and after passing through a gate you are back in the village, passing the pretty terraced cottages of North Road, called The Row when they were built for the quarry workers. The largest building was one of Pentewan's three limekilns. **On reaching the harbour turn right, past the public toilets, to return to your starting-point.**

WALK 9
PORTHPEAN, CASTLE GOTHA, TRENARREN AND THE COAST

Almost five miles; or the route could be split into two round walks of about half that distance: see point 3 in the directions.

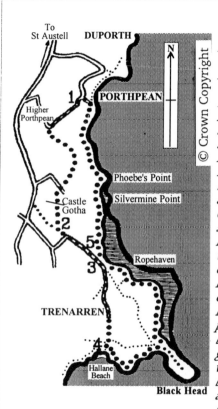

The stretch of coastline included on this walk is very beautiful, and even the inland parts of the route offer many fine views of the sea and the cliffs. The small villages of Higher Porthpean and Trenarren are both delightful, Trenarren being especially idyllic. Traces of two Iron Age fortified settlements are to be seen. This part of the coast has several steep ups and downs, so you might prefer to make two walks of it. The car park at the entrance to the Ropehaven nature reserve just above Trenarren (grid reference SX 033 489) is ideally placed for the short walk around Hallane, Black Head and Gerrans Point, and would also be a suitable base for the other short walk (Silvermine Point, Porthpean and Castle Gotha) or the complete 5-mile walk, but for these I have suggested you use the car park above Porthpean beach, because that would mean you could get refreshments at the end of the walk during the season, from the beach café. There are several small, attractive and easily accessible beaches along the way.

Porthpean ("little cove") is signposted from the St Austell bypass road (A390), about half way between the roundabouts at Mount Charles and the Asda superstore. Soon after the entrance drive to Penrice Hospital, take the left turning signposted to Porthpean beach. There is a car park just above the beach; out of season this may be closed, in which case you will need to find a roadside parking spot. Alternatively, you could drive back up to the top road (either via Higher Porthpean or back along the road you have just come down) and follow the signs to Trenarren. Just above Trenarren is a small car park, from which you could pick up the walk directions at point 3. There is no bus service to Porthpean; Charlestown, nearly a mile away via the coast path, is served by "Hoppas" from St Austell.

1 On leaving the Porthpean car park, turn right, passing the sign Higher Porthpean. The steep, narrow road soon brings you up to the pretty little village, with its attractive chapel-of-ease (St Levan's Church), spoilt only by the rusty cowl on its chimney. It was built in 1884 at the instigation of Sir Charles and Lady Graves Sawle of Penrice. (The pre-eminence of the Sawles in local society is illustrated by a story told by Canon Hammond in his history of St Austell. "A lady in one of our Sunday Schools asked a boy in her class "who was the first King of Israel?" As he did not know, she presently informed him that it was King Saul. "What, Sir Charles?" said the youth, in open-eyed astonishment.") The village square still has its old pump, but the post office indicated on the OS map is now "Post House", and the school (another gift of the Graves Sawles) is now "Old School House"; not far away are farm buildings, many of them now looking rather dilapidated and empty ... Evidently Higher Porthpean was once a lot livelier than the sleepy village we wandered through on that hot August day, where not even a cat or dog stirred, let alone a human being.

Walk past the pump, Post House and Old School House, and at the entrance to Court Cottage take the narrow path down on your left. Go through the metal kissing gate, the first of many on this walk. **Follow the obvious track that runs parallel with the cliff-edge, just a hundred yards or so above the coast path. Kissing gate 2 is in a hedge on your right, beside a Public Footpath sign; cut diagonally across the field this gate admits you to, heading just right of the farmhouse. Soon you will see another footpath sign on the skyline ahead: make for that. Cross the farm lane after negotiating kissing gate 3 and go through kissing gate 4.** (This is where I feel the kissing has to stop! From now on every gate on this walk is of the kissing variety unless otherwise stated.) **Cut across the left-hand corner of the field to gate 5, continue across the next small field to gate 6, and then still in the same direction down the much larger field to gate 7.**

At this point, before passing through gate 7, you could turn quite sharply back, at an angle of about 45° to the line you have just been walking, in order to look at the remains of Castle Gotha.

CASTLE GOTHA

Evidence from digs during the late 1950s and early 1960s suggests that this site was occupied for 300-400 years, from the second century BC to the second century AD. The people lived in stone or wooden huts, and many of them seem to have been metalworkers; there also appears to have been a workshop handling the local Pentewan stone. Most of the rampart and ditch have been ploughed out, but the oval-shaped enclosure was apparently rather more than a hundred yards across at its widest, with its entrance to the north-east. A very detailed account of the excavations at Castle Gotha was published in the 1982 issue of *Cornish Archaeology.*

Look for another kissing (sorry!) gate in a hedge, with a dry ditch curving off to the right of it. This is part of the ancient "castle"; most of the rest has disappeared beneath the plough. The view, both coastal and inland, which you get from the other side of the gate, makes it clear why our ancestors chose this site for their settlement. Return the same way to gate 7 to continue the walk.

2 Beyond that gate, walk beside the hedge on your left to gate 8, which brings you to a minor road. Here you have a delightful view to the left of a deep valley (later you'll be scaling the sides of that one, so reserve some energy!), and across to the beach at Carlyon Bay. **Continue ahead along the road**, which has high banks at first but soon gives you a superb view eastwards to Gribbin Head, not far from Fowey. **Soon you will come down to the small car park just above Trenarren,** beside the entrance to the Cornwall Trust for Nature Conservation's Ropehaven Cliffs Nature Reserve. This consists of 49 acres of cliffs and broadleaved woods in an oustandingly beautiful setting, and particularly in winter it is an excellent vantage point for observing bird life.

3 *Here you could follow the coast path sign at the near end of the parking space, thus omitting Trenarren and Black Head and reducing the walk to about two-and-a-half miles. For the shorter route back to Porthpean, pick up the directions at point 5.*

For the complete walk, continue down the road past Trenarren House, the home for many years now of the Cornish historian A.L.Rowse (created a Companion of Honour in the 1997 New Year's Honours List), and through the charming hamlet of Trenarren, whose pretty cottages were thickly bedecked with flowers when we were there. ("Adorable" is Rowse's choice of adjective for Trenarren, in "The Story of Polruddon".)

TRENARREN

The name appears to mean "Crane Castle" - or possibly "Heron Castle", since according to Oliver Padel "the two birds were not strictly distinguished in practice". The first syllable probably derives from *dyn,* a fort, rather than from *tre,* a farm or village, and presumably refers to Castle Gotha, although Black Head is closer. Once Trenarren was much larger, and had two pubs plus several shops. In his *St Austell - Church: Town: Parish* (1960), A.L.Rowse writes of the Hext family who in 1618 took up residence in the manor house in "this exquisite, sheltered valley", "a paradisal, though not particularly profitable, place to settle." They built their Georgian house, further uphill, in 1810. A photograph of it is included in the book. In *A.L.Rowse's Cornwall* (1988) he says it was built in 1805, and mentions how he "longed to live there".

When you reach the entrance to Hallane House, continue downhill on the track to the right, which soon becomes a pretty woodland path. **It's worth going on down past the coast-path signs, beside Hallane Mill to the delightful little Hallane beach** - a real sun-trap on that August day, and almost deserted. It is indeed, as Martin Collins says in his *South West Way,* "a superb picnic spot", but unfortunately it tends to be a trap for floating oil as well as sunshine, so I advise you to watch carefully where you sit. Care is required when bathing, too, because of the many submerged rocks.

4 Return to the coast path signs. If you are interested in watermills, you may care to go a few feet along the path to the left to see where the

A cottage at Trenarren

millstream crosses it; the waterwheel itself, of course, has gone. To continue the walk, however, **follow the coast path sign to the right.** Soon you are climbing quite steeply, and have a view to Pentewan beach; on reaching the stile at the top you see Black Head, and before long you will have to decide whether to walk out on to it. It would be a pity not to: the views from it are very fine. When you are near the tip you feel as if you are on a small island, and it's easy to understand why it was chosen as the site of a settlement in Iron Age times. There are traces of three lines of defence across the neck of the headland, the most obvious of them being two ramparts over 5m high and a ditch 2m deep, all on the left side of the path as you walk out. On the same side are the remains of a rifle range: two shooting platforms and a metal contraption, the target butts. It all looks as if it fell out of use many years ago, but according to the relevant National Trust leaflet (*Coast of Cornwall,* No. 20) it is still used on alternate Sundays in winter, when "due notice is given and red flags (are) flown." Something of the flavour of life in these parts over 150 years ago is captured by a short item from the *West Briton* of May 1835: "On Thursday the 14th instant, the crew of the preventive boat stationed at Porthpean, 'crept' up (trawled up with grapnels) 125 tubs of contraband spirits, sunk by smugglers, off the Blackhead, and lodged them in the custom-house sheds at Fowey."

Back to the coast path now, which ascends a short flight of steps and

Black Head

now in the distance are Porthpean beach, with a large white house, Porthpean House, above it; Duporth "holiday village" above another beach; and, a little further right, Charlestown, with its docks and spired church. The path curves left near Gerrans Point - a rather surprising name in view of the fact that Gerrans village is a good many miles southwest, near Portscatho. Perhaps this place has some association with the 8th-century Cornish "king" or chieftain, Gerent, who supposedly lived at Dingerein Castle in Gerrans parish. Now the woods of the Ropehaven nature reserve come into view, with several attractive little beaches below them. The remains of fish cellars still exist at Ropehaven, and the foundations of harbour walls can be seen at low tide. The name appears on some old maps as "Ropehawn" or even "Ropehorn". **After some steps downwards, the coast path turns left** (the path ahead leads to the first of those beaches) **and then rises quite steeply before curving inland to the small car park just above Trenarren. Cross the stile at the far end of the car park.**

5 The coast path now runs above the woods of the nature reserve, and soon goes steeply down to a bridge over a stream in a deep gully. The stream falls to a silvery little beach below.

"Silvery" came to mind because the small headland ahead is called Silvermine Point. Roger Treleaven of Trevissick, who farms most of the coastal area from Polrudden (near Pentewan) to this point, told us he had never come across any evidence of mining here; on the far side there is a cave just above high-tide level which could possibly conceal an adit (drainage channel), but I have not explored it. A.K.H. Jenkin says "an adit is known to exist at Silvermine Point", and suggests it may be a relic of Wheal Neptune, an unsuccessful attempt to mine copper between 1812 and 1821.

78 steps bring you almost to the top, where there's another stile and a good view of Porthpean beach. "Porthpean," writes Canon Hammond, "was much addicted to smuggling - many is the lugger (it is said) that has been run ashore here. The contraband goods would be carried away inland by mules, over whose track a drove of sheep would be driven to obliterate their footprints." Next comes a lovely sweep of clifftop fields; keep to the edge. Another deep valley follows, with a natural arch at Phoebe's Point. Soon you are descending towards Porthpean. *(PTO for a note about Porthpean House.)*

Porthpean House has a steep three-acre garden noted especially for its collection of two hundred camellias, as well as for its show of primroses in early spring. It is occasionally open to the public in aid of charity: for details see the current issue of the Gardens in Cornwall Open Guide. Porthpean House is owned by the Petherick family, of whom A.L.Rowse writes: "The St Austell tradition is that the founder of the family fortunes walked out of Cornwall on foot all the way to Cumberland, where he found an extremely rich tin mine and made a large fortune." (St Austell: Church - Town - Parish)

Silvermine Point

WALK 10
PAR, CARLYON BAY AND CHARLESTOWN
About six miles; nearly eight if extended to Porthpean.
Could be done as a walk of three to four miles, returning to Par by bus.

I hesitated about including this in the book, mainly because of the difficulty of making a satisfactory "round walk" of it: the area immediately inland is quite heavily built up or occupied by private woodland and a golf course, and threaded through with busy roads and the main railway line. I also supposed that the coast here was rather unexciting, and spoilt by modern industry and large-scale "leisure" complexes. On the other hand, to leave out Charlestown would have been unthinkable ... So my wife and I dutifully set off from Par on a clear, crisp October morning, and enjoyed the coastal walking far more than we had dared to hope: it is full of variety, provides superb views both along the coast and inland, and if it is less dramatic than other sections it atones by being less strenuous. Charlestown did not disappoint: its very special magic can best be appreciated from the coast path, if not from a boat. The problem of the return route remained, and I am not wholly satisfied with the one I am about to offer, because too much of the first part is on roads, and the rest is the same as the end of Walk 11. The views from that particular stretch are very fine, however, and there are compensating factors even on the earlier inland section. Even so, you may prefer to walk back along the coast or use public transport: the St Austell Hoppa Service No. 31 links Charlestown and Par. See the current timetables. Par and Charlestown have pubs and shops, and during the season refreshments can be obtained at the "Cornish Leisure World" and Porthpean beach.

Directions are given from the Par Inn: see the start of Walk 11, where you will also find the sketch map. East-to-west is the better direction to walk this section of the coast path unless you want to have the steaming chimneys of Par in your sights most of the time.

1 **From the Par Inn walk south, that is, along the main road to St Austell, with a railway line and the Par River on your left. Soon you pass under the main London-Penzance line,** carried by a rather unusual bridge with arches within its arches. Next come the huge ECCI "dries" with their gleaming silver stacks, and then the main entrance to Par Harbour: see the note in Walk 11. (The name "Par" itself means harbour or cove.) **Take the fenced path on the left just after the traffic lights at the second railway bridge.** Notice on the right, beyond the bridge and the road, disused china-clay dries (now used as stores) with ivy-covered stacks, and a line of circular concrete settling or de-watering tanks on the hill above them. Where the path crosses a footbridge you are close to more such tanks, some circular and others rectangular, and then you come to the edge of the golf course.

2 **On reaching the coast, it's worth going left first** for a ground-level view of the harbour. (You get a bird's-eye view later if you do the full round walk.) On the seaward side of Treffry's great breakwater is Spit Point, a Mecca for lovers of rock pools. **Return the same way for the walk to Charlestown,** starting above Spit Beach along low cliffs of silvery slate which are quite rapidly being eroded. The view ahead now, if it's clear enough, stretches to Chapel Point, just past Mevagissey, with a glimpse of the Dodman above it; closer is Black Head; Porthpean and Duporth beaches can be seen, but not yet Charlestown harbour. The Carlyon Bay Hotel is prominent. Inland are St Austell and, closer, St Blazey Gate (Biscovey) with its spired church. Gradually the cliffs, with small quarries scooped out here and there (though some of the cavities may result from natural cliff-falls), become higher as you walk above the long Crinnis (*) Beach.

CRINNIS

It is almost unbelievable now that the area around the Carlyon Bay Hotel was for a few years the site of one of the world's most productive copper mines: Crinnis, later called Great Crinnis, or Great Crinnis and Carlyon Consolidated. When it was started in earnest, in 1811, it was called Crinnis Cliff Mine: the adit (drainage channel) opened out at the foot of the cliffs, and some mining was carried out under the sea. The OS map indicates a disused shaft close to the cliff edge a little way west of the hotel; but the workings extended inland at least as far as Crinnis Wood, where rather more extensive remains are indicated. Some prospecting had been done in the area a little earlier, and Captain Joseph Michell, whom Jenkin describes as "an experienced and reputable miner", is now best remembered for stating in 1808 that the property was "not worth a pipe of baccy". By October 1812 the mine was producing about 600 tons of rich ore per month; in 1813 25-30 pack mules were employed carrying ore down to Charlestown harbour: "no such mine was ever known before in Cornwall," declared a newspaper correspondent at that time. One of its exceptional features was that the great body of ore lay quite close to the surface. This proved a mixed blessing: an article in *Mining Journal* reported that "the various offices of the establishment sunk to the depth of many fathoms, giving the appearance of an earthquake."

The mine's success was short-lived. Trouble was brewing by about 1818 when the various adventurers (shareholders) who had lost interest before 1811 began trying to lay claim to a share of the huge profits: see the interesting extract from the *West Briton* of 3 April 1818, included in *Life in Cornwall in the Early Nineteenth Century,* Bradford Barton 1970. Legal actions went on for years, involving also the neighbouring East Crinnis mine, over which the Duchy of Cornwall claimed mineral rights. (It is said that in that action, documents weighing three-quarters of a ton were brought in evidence, and that the 130 witnesses consumed "370 grogs and 50 bottles of wine" on one evening alone.)

Well before these matters were settled, the best lodes at Great Crinnis had been worked out; the mine struggled on for a few more years before closing; Jenkin and Barton seem to disagree about the date of closure. Further attempts to work it were made in the 1850s and 1870s, but with little success. By the period when A.L.Rowse's mother was a child - presumably about 1870 - many of the old workings of Crinnis were already out of sight and out of mind. She told him "of the tennis party given at Crinnis House (where a younger generation of Carlyons was living at the time), in the course of which the tennis lawn collapsed, there being a shaft beneath. Then there was the neighbouring farm of Mrs Hicks's, where they had all been to help about the hayrick which was constructed for shelter right beside the house. Next morning, when they got up, it had disappeared - also down a shaft." *(A Cornish Childhood)*

Inland, notice the seat of the Carlyon family, Tregrehan, among woods: see the note in Walk 11. Now you are entering the realm of the "Cornish Leisure World", "The Entertainment Capital of the West". As you approach the vast warehouse-like building which is the beating heart of that great enterprise (though there have been a few cardiac arrests lately), keep to the edge of the golf course until a sign directs you further left. **When you reach the road**, unless you feel irresistibly drawn to your left **continue over the zebra crossing, beside the car park, and across the mown greensward that decorates the view from the Carlyon Bay Hotel. (The official path presumably keeps to the right-hand edge.)** Just before the path briefly joins Sea Road opposite the Porth Avallen Hotel there is a good view-point on the left, from which you can get your first glimpse of Charlestown harbour. The nearest headland is called Appletree Point; not a likely-looking spot for fruit-growing, but Cyril Bunn mentions a local saying that the white monks who once owned land in this area had an orchard here. Somewhat later than the monks' day it was mined, mainly for copper; Dines's short note on Appletree or South Crinnis Mine refers to "extensive old workings", "said to reach 100 fms. below adit" - that is, 600 feet below the drainage shaft, the portal of which is presumably in the cliff just above high-tide level. Records of the mine's output cover the period 1849-66.

Now follow the acorn signs, and soon you are descending towards Charlestown. The stack inland is part of the Charlestown Lower Dry, now disused. There are toilets just above the harbour. The Rashleigh Arms is a short way inland, not far beyond the Shipwreck & Heritage Centre.

CHARLESTOWN

In 1790 this was a fishing village (total population: 9 persons), known as Porthmear, Polmear, or West Polmear to avoid confusion with Polmear north of Polkerris. There was no harbour, but already some china clay was being shipped from the beach: in that year, for example, four vessels bringing in coal and limestone and taking china clay and china stone had suffered damage in the process.

Twelve months later, a period of rapid change had begun, as a result of the enterprise of Charles Rashleigh. Born in 1747 at Menabilly (the mansion near Gribbin Head that was to become the home of Daphne du Maurier) and trained as a lawyer, he settled at Duporth (with a town house in St Austell, now the White Hart Hotel) as a successful businessman with interests in china-clay and mining. Armed with plans he had commissioned the famous engineer John Smeaton to draw, he first had a pier built, and then over the next few years thousands of tons of rock were excavated to make room for two basins, a dry dock, warehouses, a ship-building yard and dwellings. A hotel, a rope manufactory, cooperages, limekilns, a brickworks and pilchard seines soon followed, and Rashleigh had a four-gun battery erected on the cliffs to the south for protection during the French wars. One of his most interesting achievements was to obtain a supply of water for his dock basins by building a leat from the Luxulyan Valley. About six miles long, it passes over an aqueduct and through several tunnels, and the cost of its construction and upkeep was met partly by using it to power watermills along the way. The leat can still be seen at the northern end of the Treffry Viaduct (see Walk 12 in *Around the River Fowey)*, and is crossed by the Saints' Way just south of Trevanney farm. See also Walk 12 in this book.

The population of what was soon renamed Charlestown in honour of its creator had reached nearly 3,000 by 1851. A press advert in 1817 referred to "Charlestown from whence all the china clay raised in Cornwall is shipped", but at first it was mostly the copper mines like Crinnis that kept the port busy, and a foundry was set up in the village mainly in order to supply them with shovels, kibbles, pumps, waterwheels, engines and boilers; as the mines declined the china-clay industry grew, so the foundry turned to supplying equipment for that. As Charlestown Engineering it still flourishes. In 1908 John Lovering built a dry close to the dock, to process liquid clay piped from his pits at Carclaze. The dried clay was stored in the building which now houses the Shipwreck & Heritage Centre; from there a tramway took it to the dockside via the tunnel still clearly visible.

The dock was always too small for comfort, and as the ships grew in size so the trade moved to Par and Fowey (and to some extent Pentewan, though that had problems of its own, as described elsewhere in this book), but coasters of up to 500 tons still use the port, and we were lucky enough to see one come in recently. Liz Luck in *South Cornish Harbours* gives an excellent description of this delicate operation.

A china-clay vessel entering Charlestown dock

"Tall ships" are often to be seen at Charlestown, sometimes in connection with the making of films, many of which have used Charlestown as a setting. An occasional visitor used to be the beautiful brig "Maria Asumpta", built in Spain in 1858, rebuilt in 1981-2 and tragically smashed to matchwood off The Rumps, near Padstow, in May 1995.

During the past twelve years, ownership of the Charlestown Estate has changed hands several times, raising fears of unsympathetic commercial development. So far there have been no drastic changes, but as Richard and Bridget Larn, joint Curators of the Shipwreck & Heritage Centre, write at the end of their major history of Charlestown (see below), "without question the port ... has to produce revenue if it is to survive ... and some change is inevitable."

For more about this fascinating place, visit the Centre, which has produced its own booklet, *The Story of Charlestown.* Since *Around St Austell* was published three books about Charlestown have appeared, all of them during 1994. Two of them are by the Larns: a brief but very well illustrated one in the Tor Mark series, simply entitled *Charlestown,* and a much fuller study in hardback published by the authors, *Charlestown, The History of a Cornish Seaport.* The third is one of Peter Bray's many books of old photographs, *Around and About Charlestown.*

3 It's well worth continuing along the coast path, even if only for the views of Charlestown which you get near the start. Part-way up the fairly steep climb there is an excellent vantage-point for watching china-clay vessels inching their way round the impossibly-tight-looking corners at the entrance to the dock. Beyond the first two kissing gates there is a good view of the old china-clay dry. After the third gate the path runs through woodland above Du Porth beach. The name means "two coves" or "two harbours", presumably referring to "big harbour" (West Polmear, Charlestown) and "little harbour" (Porthpean). A bridge takes the coast path above the lane linking the Duporth Holiday Resort to its beach. The Georgian Duporth House was built by Charles Rashleigh as his country home. Its grounds were described in 1882 as an "earthly paradise". "It is all now," acidly comments Dr Rowse, "quite appropriately to the age *we* live in, a holiday camp."

In the woods above Carrickowel ("high rock") Point beside the blue notice about dogs on beaches there is a path to the road which would provide a possible return route to Charlestown, but it is a good deal longer than the coastal walk and is entirely on roads which tend to be busy. The road down into Charlestown is, however, attractive, especially the lower end of it. It enters the village almost opposite the pub.

As the coast path runs down to Porthpean beach there is a garden area with seats on the left, and a short way below that is an unusual little concrete building, a World War II watch-house. The final descent is by quite a steep flight of steps. **Unless you want to continue to Black Head (Walk 9), return to Charlestown by the same route or the alternative I have mentioned; and at Charlestown if you are walking rather than bussing back to Par, start by retracing your steps along the coast.**

4 **Where the path joins Sea Road, for the inland route continue on the road.** This makes quite pleasant walking: it is evidently a "select" residential area, with well-kept gardens and what John Betjeman would probably call "villas". **At the end of it, after passing the Carlyon Bay Hotel, you could return to the coast path by going down the road on the right which leads to the "Leisure World", or to stay inland continue ahead along the private road which has the golf links on the right and soon passes under the main railway line.** The bridge, built in 1859, is in the "Gothick" style, perhaps in deference to the wishes of the Squire at the time - a Carlyon, presumably.

5 **On joining the main Par - St Austell road (A3082), turn right.** Luckily there is a pavement to use.

6 **Take the first left turning, Pennys Lane, an attractive little country road. Just beyond a long, low bungalow (Lilac Cottage), turn right on to a grassy track. Continue ahead through the kissing gate.** On the far side of the field you now enter are a disused mine shaft and ruins of buildings including the base of a large pumping-engine house, relics of New Pembroke Mine(*). **The path passes through another kissing gate and then over an old wooden stile.**

7 **Turn left at the road (Biscovey Road), then first right, St Mary's Road. For the rest of the walk, see section 8 in Walk 11.**

NEW PEMBROKE MINE

This name was adopted in 1863 when Pembroke Mine, which had during the 1820s been nearly as productive of copper as Crinnis, was reopened. By 1870, New Pembroke had a work-force of about 130, and the engine house whose base still lurks among the vegetation was built about then for a very large (80-inch) pumping engine, which when built by Harveys of Hayle in 1839 had the longest stroke of any engine in Cornwall, twelve feet. This engine provides an example of the way such machinery moved from site to site: she had worked at the Wheal Treasure section of Fowey Consols until 1846 (see Walk 11 in *Around the River Fowey*), then went to another of Treffry's mines, Par Consols; she was bought by New Pembroke in 1869, and a few years after the closure of this mine in 1876 she migrated to her last home, a lead mine near Holywell in North Wales. (Like a ship, a Cornish beam engine is always "she", never "it".) Kenneth Brown, who provided me with most of the above information, says, "It is of interest that she was far too big for the needs of New Pembroke so the mine next door (near where the DIY centre now is) prevailed upon the adventurers to run flat-rods from the 80 to drain their shaft - one of very few cases in Cornish mining history where adventurers in one mine paid another to keep their water out!" (Flat-rods were horizontal iron or occasionally wooden rods used to transfer power from an engine or waterwheel to a remote location.)

WALK 11
PAR, ST BLAZEY & BISCOVEY
with a possible extension to PONTS MILL
Nearly four miles, plus nearly two miles with the extension

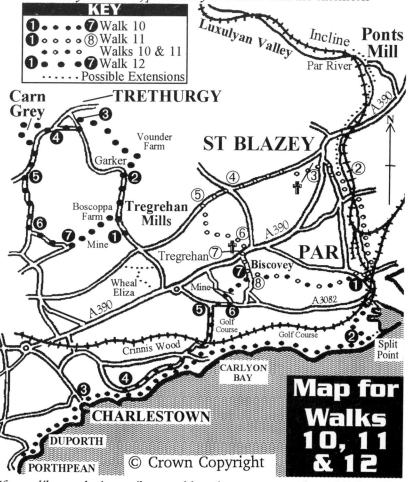

KEY
❶ • • • • ❼ Walk 10
❶ ○ ○ ○ ○ ⑧ Walk 11
• ○ • ○ • ○ Walks 10 & 11
❶ • • • ❼ Walk 12
· · · · · · Possible Extensions

Carn Grey
TRETHURGY
Luxulyan Valley
Incline
Ponts Mill
Par River
ST BLAZEY
Vounder Farm
Garker
Boscoppa Farm
Tregrehan Mills
Mine
Tregrehan
Biscovey
PAR
Wheal Eliza
Mine
Golf Course
Golf Course
Crinnis Wood
CARLYON BAY
Split Point

© Crown Copyright

Map for Walks 10, 11 & 12

CHARLESTOWN
DUPORTH
PORTHPEAN

If you like exploring railways old and new, or canals and other water engineering works, or old mining areas, this walk will be a "must" for you; if not, you would still enjoy it for its beauty and variety: an ancient church, country paths and minor roads in delightful wooded valleys and along ridges with some fine panoramic views of the coast - these are just a few of the pleasures in store. It's quite an easy walk, but you are likely to encounter mud in the valleys near Tregrehan and Ponts Mill, and a stick to deal with vegetation might prove useful on the path above St Blazey church. Pubs and shops are conveniently placed at Par, St Blazey and Biscovey (St Blazey Gate), and there are public toilets at St Blazey football ground.

The Par Inn (grid reference SX 075536) seems to be the logical start/end point, and I'm told the food there is particularly good, especially Mrs Dingle's pasties. Roadside parking nearby isn't usually hard to find; to drive there from St Austell or Truro, drive east on the A390 and turn right towards Fowey on the A3082. As you approach Par the road passes under two railway bridges close to a big china-clay works, and then the Par Inn is on the left immediately beyond the right turning to Fowey and Par. Several bus and train services link St Austell and Par. A good alternative start/end would be near the St Blazey AFC ground (SX 070547). To drive there, continue along the A390 as far as St Blazey church and turn sharp-right there towards Par. The football ground is a short way along on the left, and there are car parks both beside it and a little further along the road, also on the left. Turn to the end of point 2 in the directions if you are starting there.

1 From the Par Inn walk a few yards along the road almost opposite, signposted to Par and Fowey. You immediately cross a small leat or canalised stream, then the railway line; next comes the Par or Luxulyan River, also canalised, and finally the remains of Treffry's Par Canal, now part of a scheme to reduce the risk of flooding at Par and St Blazey.

THE PAR CANAL

Joseph Thomas Austen (1782-1850) took over Fowey Consols mine (on the hill on the east side of Tywardreath Highway) in 1822, and under his control it soon became one of the world's greatest copper mines.

The problems involved in transporting the ore to Fowey along the primitive roads prompted him to try a typically daring and imaginative solution: to build a harbour at Par, to get the ore down into the valley a little way south of Ponts Mill by building a tramway on an inclined plane, and to construct a canal linking the two.

By the mid-1830s the system was operating. A completely new channel was cut for the Par River, a little to the west of its original course, and the old riverbed was widened and deepened sufficiently to accommodate barges carrying 52 tons of ore, drawn by horses. Three locks, each ninety feet long, were constructed. Later, two more inclined planes from the mine were built, and the canal was extended to Ponts Mill in order to link up with the new tramway Treffry was building through the Luxulyan Valley to serve his quarries and china-clay pits - and eventually, he hoped, to reach his other harbour at Newquay.

The business of transferring goods between canal barges and wagons at the foot of the Carmears Incline proved costly in time and labour, and Austen (who in 1838 changed his surname to Treffry, his mother's maiden name - pronounced Tre-fry) planned to replace the canal with a further tramway. In 1855, five years after Treffry's death, this was built; the canal fell out of use, and, to quote the Cornwall Archaeological Unit's report, "There is now little to distinguish the route of the Canal from any other small stream in the area."

Its course at the northern end can be traced on the map by following the parish boundary; south of the A390 it ran very close to the canalised river: the new flood-prevention channel is actually the old canal.

For the walk, take the track which runs on the left side of this last waterway, passing a few houses at first. Soon it becomes a grassy track. Over to the left you have a good view of some of the rather grand brick buildings erected in 1874 as locomotive sheds and engineering works for the Cornwall Minerals Railway but now serving mostly as garages or for storage. This complex includes the UK's only surviving "half-moon" locomotive roundhouse, and is scheduled. The track you are on, formerly the towpath of Treffry's canal, marks the course of the mineral line built in 1855: this is evident from the row of substantial granite "setts" (sleeper blocks), very similar to those in the Luxulyan Valley (see *Around the River Fowey,* Walk 12). Now the river is close, on the left. Cross the Newquay loop-line with due care and attention. The modern railway line runs on the far side of the river for a little way, then crosses back just before the road at Middleway. (The change in the landscape here over the past two centuries is illustrated by the fact that "A map of Roselyon, dated 1794, shows a stream-work then in operation at Middleway ... with a ship under sail passing close alongside." [A.K.H. Jenkin:*Mines and Miners of Cornwall]*)

When you reach the road, go left, over the level crossing, and then continue on the riverside path, now called Rundles Walk. On the hillside ahead are the old woods of Prideaux (pronounced "Priddix" in these parts, though not in Padstow), together with newer plantations of conifers at the southern end of the Luxulyan Valley.

2 Nearby on the left now you will see St Blazey church, and the path along the left end of the football pitch makes a convenient short cut to it, so the time has come to decide whether to extend the walk to Ponts Mill, the point where Treffry's canal ended and the mineral line rose by a steep incline to the level of the magnificent viaduct Treffry built in the Luxulyan Valley. (If you do not want to walk there now, turn left beside the pitch and pick up the directions where bold type resumes, at the end of the section in italics that follows.)

For Ponts Mill (*), continue beside the river. Still running beside it are the Newquay line and the flood-prevention waterway. The large old building with four arched openings is a set of limekilns, though adapted now to other purposes. On the left beside the A390 is the former site of Moon's Aberdeen Laundry, whose stone stack used to be a local landmark. The laundry operated for nearly a century (1889-1983), employing up to about a hundred people.

(I should warn you that from here on, the suggested route is not a right of way; most of it is owned by English China Clays International. I understand from people I have spoken to in Par that it has been a popular walk for many years; ECCI are happy for its unofficial use to continue, but walkers who use it do so on their own responsibility. Particular care must be taken at the Ponts Mill end, where railway lines still in use have to be crossed.)

Cross the main road with care and continue on the left side of the river. Eventually the path passes under the railway line and then over the river, and you soon realise you are walking along the course of an old two-foot-gauge railway or tramway: see Vaughan page 73 and Plate 114. This linked the

Prideaux Wood china-clay kiln to the Cornwall Mineral Railways line, and was probably used only by horse-drawn wagons. Nearby is a sadly battered concrete building labelled "The New Consolidated Mines of Cornwall Ltd" (built about 1920 as a power station for the St Austell Electric Light and Power Company), and sluice gates have been set up to control the water in the river. At this point, cross with due care the railway lines that lead into and beside the china-clay works (the lines may look disused, but see Mr Vaughan's photo No. 115, taken in January 1991), and continue along the narrow road which runs beside a rusty siding and the river. On the right at the point where the siding ends was one of the basins at the terminus of the Par Canal, now choked up and almost unrecognisable.

Soon you reach a road which leads left into the china-clay works. The bridge it crosses was built about 1836 to span the diverted river and also the new canal. Above the bridge was another basin where 60-ton canal barges were loaded; in 1991 construction work for the flood prevention scheme was going on here. Notice on the north side of the bridge an iron launder, built to carry back to the river the water from one of the leats in the Luxulyan Valley.

PONTS MILL

By the end of the 12th century, Tywardreath Priory had set up a corn mill here, at a time when this was the lowest bridging point on the Par River (hence the name) and the highest point of navigation. 80-ton vessels could still reach Ponts Mill over 500 years later; but by 1800 the river had brought down vast quantities of silt caused by tin streaming, and when basins for the canal were dug out in 1835 medieval bridges were found 25 feet below the surface. The story of industrial developments at Ponts Mill over the last two centuries, involving hydraulic engineering, tramways and railways, mining, quarrying, china-clay and china-stone processing, forestry and probably much else, is far too complex for me to attempt to tell here. The best account of it I have come across is in *The Luxulyan Valley,* published by the Cornwall Archaeological Unit in 1988. Also good, despite irritating errors like referring to Treffry's great mine as "Fowey Consuls", is John Vaughan's *The Newquay Branch and its Branches* (1991), which includes excellent photographs.

If you continue walking in the same line as before and take the left fork in the (muddy) track, you will soon reach a wooden stile and a stone bridge at the foot of the Carmears Incline, with granite setts clear to see. The long climb from here to the site of the Carmears waterwheel is very worthwhile if you have the time and energy for it .... and then, of course, you can tack on Walk 12 from Around the River Fowey! But to complete the walk back to Par, return the same way as far as the St Blazey football ground and turn right towards the church.

At the road turn right *(but see the note in italics which follows),* **and at the A390 cross to St Blazey church (*).** If you find it locked you should be able to borrow a key from the Cornish Arms.

NOTE: If you are particularly interested in industrial history, turn left first to see the remains of William West's St Blazey Foundry. The surviving buildings are now used by Smith and Treffry, builders' merchants. West was one of the great engineers, noted particularly for his work at Fowey Consols.

He set up this foundry, conveniently close to the canal, in 1848, and for several decades following it was St Blazey's biggest employer. The foundry carried out repair and maintenance work for the mines and built many important beam engines. Five cast-iron road bridges built here in 1873 can still be seen in the Roche area, spanning the Par-Newquay branch line. West died in 1879 and his sons carried on the business for a further fourteen years; after a short period under the ownership of R.Liddicoat & Sons, the foundry closed in about 1900. Kenneth Brown has written about the St Blazey Foundry in the 1991 issue of the Journal of the Trevithick Society, which includes a photograph by him of the curved wall on one side of the entrance, necessary to manoeuvre engine beams and other long loads into the narrow street. Further details about West and his career are in Valerie Brokenshire's book - see the note below.

ST BLAZEY AND ITS CHURCH

The old name for the village was Landreath or Landreth, "church-place by the beach"; nearby are Tywardreath, "house upon the beach", and Treesmill, "the mill by the beach". Look where they are on the map: there is no better example in Cornwall, or probably anywhere, of the dramatic effects river-borne detritus can have on a landscape. "That the sea has been driven back from S. Blazey Bridge for at least two miles, within memory, is an indisputable fact," wrote Joseph Polsue (1867); as recently as 1842, Cyrus Redding had written, "the road in one place almost touches upon the head of Tywardreath Bay, by Par Creek, near the church of St Blazey." Saint Blaise, according to legend, disembarked here, but what a 4th-century Armenian bishop would have been doing so far from home is hard to say. Blaise is said to have been tortured to death with a woolcomb and was therefore adopted as the patron saint of weavers and woolcombers; this village has traditionally been associated with the woollen industry, so that seems a more likely explanation of the church's dedication.

The church key - an impressive object in itself - can be obtained from the nearby pub. The building, which dates from the 15th century, had a north aisle added in 1839, and was restored in 1897, when the plaster was removed, exposing the attractive silvery granite. There are numerous memorials to members of the Carlyon family (see the note on Tregrehan), but the most prominent and unusual monument commemorates Henry Scobell, "the first Treasurer & Paymaster for ye farm Tyn to Queen Ann".

Not buried here but requiring at least a mention is Ralph Allen (1693-1764), the son of a St Blazey innkeeper, who introduced important improvements in the postal service and is said to have earned an average of nearly £12,000 per year for 42 years as a result. He built himself an impressive house near Bath, where he was also involved in quarrying; the Mansion House in Truro is faced with Bath stone which he gave as a wedding present when his niece married Thomas Daniell.

A very detailed and well illustrated history, *A Parish Portrait, St Blazey* by Valerie Brokenshire, was published by the author in 1993.

3 From the church continue the walk by going up Duke Street (beside the church gate) and straight on along the signed footpath. From up here you can get an impression of what this area looked

St Blazey from the path above the church

like when the sea lapped up to the churchyard walls: turn the football pitch and recreation ground blue! **The shady, sunken path goes up beside a derelict building.** After the first gate the path tends to become overgrown, but the landowner had recently had it cleared when I last walked it, late in 1996. **Beyond the second gate, keep straight on beside the hedge.** The view back on the right from here shows the course of the river and railway up into the Luxulyan Valley, and the scene is dominated by Austen's engine house (Fowey Consols mine): see *Around the River Fowey*, Walk 11. **Continue ahead through the farm gate and along the minor road.** At the top of the slope is Cornhill Farm, with a good view north across Bodelva Moor (though the flooded pits of the Bodelva china-clay works are not visible from this side of the valley) to Warren Wood and the Prideaux hill fort, below which runs the Saints' Way. Bodelva Pit is the site chosen for what has been called "the world's biggest greenhouse", a botanical research centre capable of housing full-grown rainforest trees. Behind the scheme is Tim Smit: see the note about Heligan in Walk 6. The estimated cost of the "Eden Project" is £110 million, about half of which will, it is hoped, come from Millennium funding.

4 At the crossroads go straight on, along the minor road signposted to Tregrehan and St Austell. This brings you down to the attractive wooded valley of Carvear Moor. The small stack and ruined buildings on the right are relics of a dry that belonged to the Carvear china-clay works. The pit which originally supplied clay to it is now part of the Bodelva pit.

5 Take the signed footpath to St Blazey Gate, on the left. This delightful - if at times rather muddy - path runs close to a little stream which flows from the china-clay workings and has deposited sand - a miniature example of the kind of silting which afflicted the Fal, the St Austell River and others in this area. I'm told that this path is known locally as Whitewater

Lane. **On reaching the edge of the grounds of Tregrehan, the path or track curves left, uphill,** and gives glimpses of the sea as you approach the main road near Par Parish Church at St Blazey Gate.

TREGREHAN

The manor of Tregrehan was part of the property of Henry Bodrugan which passed to the Edgcumbes after the Wars of the Roses: see the note about Bodrugan's Leap, Walk 5. In the 17th century Tregrehan Barton was bought by the Carlyon family, who in the opinion of the historian Hals were probably descended from "Richard Curlyon, alias King Richard I". The present mansion was built in the 18th century and "almost rebuilt within the last twenty years" according to Lake's *Parochial History* (1867).

Canon Hammond in his history of St Austell remarks that "The house and grounds are undermined in almost every direction by the workings of Old Crinnis Copper Mine." He could also have mentioned Wheal Eliza and West Par Consols; D.B.Barton mentions that very long levels had to be driven because the Carlyon family banned all shafts and surface workings on their grounds, "save on a penalty of £10,000".

Work on laying out the grounds began early last century, and improvements and replantings have continued to the present day. An account written in 1916 said that Tregrehan stood out "above all the Cornish gardens for the richness and health of its conifers"; some of those conifers are now probably the largest specimens of their species in the country. The garden is now also famous for its trees from the southern hemisphere, especially New Zealand, and the camellias planted by Miss Gillian Carlyon during this century. In recent years it has been open to the public on certain days. In 1995 these were Wednesdays to Sundays from mid-March to the end of June and again in September; please check in the current *Gardens of Cornwall Open Guide.*

You could include a visit on this walk, but unfortunately that would involve another half-mile or more on the main road: the entrance is opposite the Stadium (Great Mills etc.), just before the Britannia Inn and the turning to Fowey (A3082). There is a pavement all the way, on the left side of the road. After visiting Tregrehan, if you did decide to walk it, you could reduce the main-road stint by turning right on Pennys Lane and joining the route of Walk 10 a little way into point 6.

The name, by the way, is pronounced "Tregrain", and may mean "wrinkles estate" - work that one out if you can! A.L. Rowse, however, states that it means "hamlet on gravel". For a particularly vivid description of the house and grounds during the late 19th and early 20th centuries, see the last part of Chapter III in *A Cornish Childhood.*

6 You reach the main road close to shops and a pub, The Four Lords - whose name probably refers to the four main local landowners, Edgcumbe, Rashleigh, Carlyon and Treffry. (So suggests H.L.Douch, but Canon Hammond in his history of St Austell lists "four lords" as Edgcumbe, Tremayne and two branches of the Sawle family.) **Turn right.**

St Mary's Church, built to the designs of G.E.Street in 1849, is described enthusiastically by Betjeman in his *Shell Guide* to Cornwall. Nikolaus Pevsner wrote (in 1950) of its "pink stone which looks mellow and loveable after 100 years," and thought it "aesthetically more pleasing even than Truro Cathedral." In the churchyard, beside the small door at the south-east end of the church, is "The Biscovey Stone", which probably dates from the 10th century. It was moved here in 1896, having previously served as a gate-post for the toll gate nearby, on the main road. A.G.Langdon, in *Old Cornish Crosses*, complained bitterly of this "illustration of the apathy and want of interest in Cornwall towards its many priceless relics"; his book was published in 1896 ... Langdon gives a very full description of this cross shaft, which is beautifully decorated though much eroded, and is inscribed ALRORON ULLICI (or ULCUI?) FILIUS.

7 Turn left opposite the church, down Biscovey Road *(but see the note on Tregrehan for the possibility of extending the walk to there)*. The name, sometimes shown on old maps and documents as "Boscovey", means "house of Covey" (or a similar surname). It is pronounced "Bis-ca-vay".

8 Take the second turning on the left, St Mary's Road, and then the first right, Hillside Avenue. This becomes a path running between hedges at first, and then opening up to give wonderful views over St Austell Bay, with the golf links and the main railway line fairly close. Just down the slope below the infants' school is East Crinnis Farm, the site of a very productive copper mine of the same name, which between 1820 and 1841 was controlled by John Taylor: see Walk 14, the note on Polgooth Mine. In the valley, successful tin-streaming enterprises called Sandrycock and Porth, dating back to the mid-18th century, were carried on; interesting details about them are given by A.K. Hamilton Jenkin in *Mines and Miners of Cornwall*, Vol. XIV (pages 19-21). **A surfaced track or drive brings you past the impressive buildings of Trenovissick Farm;** a short way beyond that, the steaming chimneys of the clay dries at Par come into view; **and then you pass among the mobile homes of the Mount Holiday Park.** This area was mined by Par Consols.

PAR CONSOLS

This group of old mines was reopened about 1834, and like Fowey Consols was controlled by J.T.Treffry until his death in 1850. During the 1840s it was one of the most productive copper mines in Cornwall, employing at least eight steam engines: three for pumping, two for winding, two for stamps - one of which drove a set of a hundred heads - and a small one used to power a sawmill and also to raise and lower skips or wagons on an inclined plane down to Par harbour. In the 1850s tin gradually became the mine's main product, and for a while it was the second biggest tin-producer in the county. A man-engine was installed in 1855, one of the few designed by the St Blazey engineer William West under licence. (For more about man-engines see the notes on Tresavean Mine in *A Second View from Carn Marth* and the first volume of *Exploring Cornwall's Tramway Trails.*) By the 1860s the mine had as many as fifteen engines at work - and yet the slump in tin prices around 1865 was so bad that the whole operation closed down in 1867. Kenneth Brown informs me that one engine of special interest at Par Consols was a rare 72-inch pumping engine converted by Edward ("Ned") Bull from a two-cylinder Sims combined engine: the cylinder was inverted over the shaft.

On the edge of the "Adventure Playground" is the base of the engine house for a steam whim (winding engine); the base of the stack has, in Kenneth Brown's words, "been turned into a tasteful litter bin!" It's worth walking across the rough ground on the right for the view of Par Harbour. On the left near the exit from the Holiday Park is part of another engine house, the impressive bob-wall on which pivoted the beam or bob of Treffry's North 80-inch pumping engine. This is the engine mentioned in the note about New Pembroke Mine, Walk 10. **Continue down the road through a bungalow estate, and soon you are back at the Par Inn.**

PAR HARBOUR

Plans for a harbour at Par were drawn up in 1792. John Smeaton of Eddystone Lighthouse fame, who had designed Charlestown harbour, was involved in producing these plans, and when James Rendell was employed in 1828 by J.T.Austen (Treffry) to design Par harbour, many of Smeaton's suggestions were adopted. Rendell and Austen agreed that it should be built behind the shelter of Spit Point. Soon the two men quarrelled and Austen then took over sole responsibility for the project. Despite great problems caused by wayward currents and shifting sands, by 1830 the work was well advanced, and by the mid-1840s there were not only a southern breakwater 1,200 feet long and an even longer northern wall, together enclosing enough quayside space for over 50 ships, but smelters for tin, copper, silver and lead, a brickworks, facilities for cutting and dressing granite and for handling china clay and china stone, limekilns, ship-repair and ship-building yards, blacksmiths' and carpenters' shops, a flour mill, a pilchard fishery, and even a factory where miners' candles were made. Now, of course, the focus is entirely on china clay, and as a clay port Par is second in importance only to Fowey, which can handle large vessels even at low tide.

WALK 12
TREGREHAN MILLS, CARN GREY
AND BOSCOPPA
Just over three miles.
For the sketch-map see the start of Walk 11.

---

*This walk is something special: beautiful almost every inch of the way
(the main exception being a few hundred yards through a housing estate:
a good many inches there, I must admit), and full of historical interest. I
suppose the glorious views are what most people would remember above
all, but equally appealing to me was the pleasure of discovering half-
hidden and unexpected relics of old mines and clay works. (Please
note, however, that such sites are usually privately owned, and that to
explore them may be physically dangerous.) It's quite an easy walk,
although there are a few fairly stiff climbs - notably, of course, to the top
of Carn Grey - and a good many muddy patches in a typical Cornish
November, which is when I walked it. About a mile of the route is along a
moderately busy main road, but to my surprise this made very pleasant
walking, being downhill all the way and blessed with wonderful views
ahead. There is no shop along the way, but the post office / store at
Tregrehan Mills is close, and so are the shops at Boscoppa. The nearest
pub I know of is the Britannia Inn, almost opposite the entrance to
Tregrehan on the A390. By the way, if you have a copy of Rowse's* A
Cornish Childhood *and it's not too heavy or too precious to take out on a
walk, bring it along and read the relevant part of Chapter VIII as you
stand at the top of Carn Grey!*

The walk begins and ends at Tregrehan Mills (*), which is signposted from
the A390, on the left a short way before the roundabout at the junction with
the A3082 if you are coming from St Austell. Continue ahead over the
crossroads and past the post office. Roadside parking is rather limited but
should normally be possible opposite the playing field. Western National
bus service 24A (St Austell - Par) passes through Tregrehan village: see
current timetables.

TREGREHAN MILLS
The mills have gone now, but Valerie Brokenshire's excellent little history
of the village, *A Village Portrait* (1985), explains that there were two. Mill
ponds on both sides of the road north to Trethurgy, close to where the
stream passes under it, fed a leat which ran on the far side of the present
football field, and that powered a corn mill first, then flowed on to work
a bone mill in the woods near Boscundle, on the far side of the Bethel-
Bodelva road. This mill has now been converted into a residence called
Carpenters Barn. Mrs Brokenshire says, "the mills of Tregrehan have
existed for a very long time, certainly from 1486-1906." The water in the
leat was also used at various times to work the stamps of small mines.
　　Referring to Tregonissey in *A Cornish Childhood*, A.L.Rowse writes,
"It had never produced anybody known to history, or with an approach to
a name. Tregrehan Mills even had produced a Samuel Drew." That "even"

shows how insignificant a place it was reckoned to be. Samuel Drew, born in 1765, was a "buddle boy" at a local mine at nine and apprenticed as a shoemaker about two years later. He became famous as a preacher in the Methodist Church, and also as a writer of books and articles on metaphysics: a scholar, "endowed," as his memorial says, "with a powerful intellect". A well-known history of Cornwall by Fortescue Hitchens was edited by Drew in 1824. He died in 1833.

Methodism flourishes at Tregrehan still, and Mrs Brokenshire tells me she believes the local chapel holds a record for one of the last surviving Sunday School anniversary feast days - an old tradition. It is held on the Thursday following the first Sunday in July, and features a procession, brass band, saffron buns, a public tea and sports.

1 Continue north along the road, with the stream (locally known as the river) on your right at first - rather hidden by the dreaded Japanese knotweed, but very plainly audible, at least in November. Soon the road crosses the stream, and the marshy ground on the right here marks the site of one of the two former mill ponds. A "shoot" or spring of good drinking water still issues from a pipe in the hedge near the gate to "Brookside". Beyond that comes woodland, and soon an old stack peers out from the foliage. It served a china-clay dry a short way to the south, to which it was connected by a long flue; the remains of that run beside the road for several yards. A few feet from the stack is Maudlin's Well; its name is presumably a corruption of Magdalene's, but I have seen no reference to it in books about holy wells. Valerie Brokenshire (see the note on Tregrehan Mills) writes that people used to travel long distances to use this water because of its reputation for purity, and that this well was the source of the first piped water laid on in the village. She also mentions, however, that it drained from old mine workings, so my first impression - that this was an old adit - may not be completely wrong. The workings in question were those of Tregrehan Mine or Wheal Joney, which became part of Wheal Eliza Consols. A short way up the hill behind still stands the ruined engine house, built in about 1890 for a large rotative beam engine; once it was a prominent landmark, but now trees shroud it, and it is not accessible by public footpath.

WHEAL ELIZA CONSOLS

This group of mines, some of them quite old, included Boscundle, West Par Consols, Blue Gate, New Wheal Eliza and Tregrehan Consols. (Just in case that list hasn't confused you enough, I'll add the fact that some of those mines belonged to another group called Charlestown United before Eliza Consols was formed. The many and sometimes very slight variations of names adopted by mining companies create some of the most dangerous traps for the unwary historian of Cornish mining.) From 1864, Wheal Eliza and West Par Consols had been owned by the same company, and made huge profits by exploiting a rich tin lode that lay beneath the grounds of Tregrehan Manor: see the note on Tregrehan, Walk 11. In 1884 they employed 190 workers underground and 111 at surface.

Tregrehan Mine, once known as Wheal Joney, is quite a long way north of the other mines that formed Wheal Eliza Consols, and seems to have been added to the group at a late stage: the only recorded production before this century was ten-and-a-half tons of black tin in 1889-93. According to D.B.Barton, Wheal Eliza Consols closed in 1892, having survived to a later date than any other mine in the St Austell area. In 1908 a new attempt was made to work Wheal Eliza and Tregrehan, but this lasted only till 1913. Dines says there was "practically no production" during that period, but Collins mentions 3 tons of black tin from Tregrehan in 1909, sold for £196. Kenneth Brown tells me that a lot of evidence of the work done at this period remains at Tregrehan Mine, in the area around the engine house and the main shaft higher up the hill to the east. A ruined engine house survives at the Wheal Eliza sett, and a short walk to visit it is suggested at the end of the directions).

Only a few yards further along the road is another old stack up on the right, this time clearly part of a disused china-clay dry (Vounder). Just a short way further up the road, on the left, is what the OS map calls an "aqueduct", with a sluice gate; this leat or launder passes over the stream heading westwards. In November it was gushing with rather milky water. If you're willing and able to scramble up the bank on the right you will see where the water comes from: a small waterfall now, but there was once an overhead launder feeding a waterwheel in the wheelpit. According to information supplied to Kenneth Brown by Mr John Tonkin, the wheel was working at least till the late 1920s, and drove pumps at Carvear claypit, several hundred yards to the east, by means of flat-rods running through the adit-like tunnel close by. (Carvear is now part of Bodelva pit.)

2 Where the road bends left (approaching another old clay dry, Garkar or Garker), **go up the signed Public Bridleway which soon crosses the stream.** On the right at first is the leat, and you can see where it emerges from a tunnel. This leat is of special interest, because it was built in the late 1790s by Charles Rashleigh to carry water from Cam Bridges in the Luxulyan Valley a distance of at least six miles to Charlestown; there it fed two reservoirs, and the water in them was used to keep ships in the dock afloat at low tide, and also periodically to flush sand and other waste out to sea. The system is still, I believe, in working order. For more details see the note on Charlestown (Walk 10), and also Walk 12 in *Around the River Fowey.* **Continue up the track and then turn left through a five-bar wooden gate, opposite a metal gate and just before the entrance to The Barn, Vounder ("lane") Farm. After a muddy patch, the path goes steeply uphill and then runs above a pretty valley.** Although the view is restricted compared with what is to come, it already includes much of the coast from the Gribbin to Black Head, with a glimpse of Bodelva clay works behind (the site chosen for the "Eden Project": see Walk 11) and Carn Grey ahead. A small wooden gate brings you to an ECCI parking-place; ahead, beyond a black gate, is the attractive flooded pit known as "Hennals", now a fishing pool. Turn left on the sandy road, with a small stream on the left along part of its length.

3 At the road, turn left past the Trethurgy Wesleyan Chapel. (Rowse's explanation of "Trethurgy" as "the village of the water-dog," i.e. otter, is thought by Padel to be much less likely than "farm of Devergi", a personal name.) **A short way back to Tregrehan Mills would be to**

continue down this minor road; but for Carn Grey take the first right turning, where there is a sign to Chytan Farm, and bear left at the main road.

4 Opposite Carne Grey Cottage, take the path on the right. From here there is a rather confusing choice of paths and tracks, but you just need to keep going uphill, past an impressive flooded quarry pit, to the rock-pile beside another flooded quarry pit at the top of Carn Grey.

CARN GREY

As I hinted in my introductory note to this walk, Carn (or Carne) Grey features in A.L.Rowse's autobiography, and I would not presume to try to emulate his description of the view from it or of the special magic of the place. "In whatever mood of temper or impatience I left home," he says, "I came back from Carn Grey at peace with myself, happy."

Highland areas like this were almost certainly occupied in prehistoric times, and it is hardly surprising that legends about pagan rites have attached themselves to this place: one of them avers that Bronze Age people used the flat rock on the top of the rocky outcrop for sun worship, and sculpted the stones below to make an anticlockwise stairway up to it; another assures us that between about 700 and 200 BC Phoenician traders conducted Baal-worship here - hence, according to Cyril Bunn in his *The Book of St Austell,* the nickname of "the Baal Stone" for the flat rock, and of "Baal" for the Carclaze pit. He also mentions the legend that "when St Mewan was preaching on the Carne Grey Rock, rain began to fall, and he and St Austell took shelter under the overhang of the rock." However little truth there may be in such tales, it is certain that there were at least two barrows just south of the hill, and a site only a little way north at Trethurgy was occupied by a circular earthwork which seems to have been inhabited from about 250 to 550 AD; excavations there in 1972-3 revealed the remains of five round houses and other buildings.

Why the carn is called Grey I don't know; perhaps from a personal name, or because of the colour of the rocks (compare the various headlands with names like "Caragloose", not all of which look particularly grey to me). Stone was quarried here until 1939.

The view to the south requires no comment; to the north and west it is cut off by the big Carclaze clay works, with its monitors (high-pressure hoses) at work, and its long conveyor belt taking waste to a distant tip.

CARCLAZE

The name helps to confirm the importance of this area to prehistoric man: *crucglas,* "green barrow". J.H.Collins (1912) says that according to local people the site was mined for tin as early as the reign of Henry VII. By about 1830 it was the largest and most famous openwork mine in the county. In that year the pit was said to be six acres in extent, with eight stamping mills at work, and shafts sunk 60 feet below the bottom of the pit. T.Allom's well-known "romantic" engraving of Carclaze (1831) is included by A.L.Rowse in his *St Austell,* and in coloured form by Embrey and Symes in *Minerals of Cornwall and Devon.* One of the best descriptions is that by George Henwood in *Cornwall's Mines and Miners;*

this dates from the late 1850s, by which time Carclaze was already concentrating entirely on the production of china clay. Henwood's description of the view from Carclaze is also worth reading, and makes an interesting comparison with the one by Rowse mentioned in the note on Carn Grey.

The path continues on the south side of the pit to return to the road, where you turn right. Please walk with care: the traffic can be fast here.

Gribbin Head from Carn Grey

5 Take the first left turning, signed to Bethel (named, I presume, like the Bethel at Twelveheads, from the founding of a chapel). The road, which soon takes you past the Civic Amenity Site, is called Menear Road, referring to the prehistoric menhir or longstone, six feet tall, which can be seen from gateways on the left just past the Amenity Site. **This road is rather less busy than the other, but care is still needed. Walk facing the oncoming traffic (unless you are in a large group):** it is safer, and in this case also provides you with much better views than the motorists are able to enjoy. **Eventually you descend to the edge of the modern development of St Austell known as Boscoppa,** though the original place of that name is further east. The road names on the right - Hallane, Trenarren - call to mind another walk.

6 Turn left at Killivarder Way, whose name presumably recalls a long-lost wood *(kelli,* grove). **Keep to this road till you come to a T-junction at the bottom.**

7 Turn left there, past Bishop Bronescombe primary school, over

or beside a cattle-grid, and along a rather rough but attractive
tree-lined lane. After a few hundred yards, notice the old stack a little
distance away on the right, attached to the ruins of an engine house.
Boscoppa, described by Dines as "a small mine in killas country" (that is,
where the mineral-bearing lode ran through sedimentary rock rather than
granite), is recorded as having produced 27 tons of black tin during the
1870s, and a little more from openwork in 1899. It was probably worked
by just two men. Soon you reach Boscoppa Farm, with its attractive old
outbuildings in a beautiful setting, looking towards the coast across what
was once Boscoppa Downs and Boscundle Common. (Valerie Brokenshire
writes that "Boscoppa Downs had many mines, and leading from Mr Allen's
farm at Boscoppa is a labyrinth of tunnels, adits and shafts. It is said that
when the mines were all working one could walk from Boscoppa to Crinnis
underground.") **The track goes to the left of the old ruined manor
house of Boscoppa and becomes a narrower path running through
woodland. Soon you cross a small footbridge and are back
more-or-less where you started.** The old house set back on the right as
you join the road, Kaslo Cottage, was, says Mrs Brokenshire, the count house
for Wheal Joney where the ore was assayed.

A POSSIBLE LITTLE "EXTRA": WHEAL ELIZA

Although a path runs beside the ruined engine house of this once-important
mine, it does not fit conveniently into a round walk. If you would care to
visit the site, you could park near Boscundle Lodge, which is on the right as
you drive south from Tregrehan Mills to the A390. Watch for the public
footpath sign. You may be able to park on the little bungalow estate close
by. The path runs straight ahead, uphill, and the pumping-engine house
stands among trees on the left after three or four hundred yards, where
another track forks left. The separate stack and a capped shaft are a few
yards along that track. Return the same way.

FOOTNOTE : "WHEAL JONEY"

*The following was set down by Dr J. Penderill-Church and has reached me via John Tonkin and Kenneth
Brown. I would not care to vouch for the literal truth of every colourful detail, but in essence it may reflect
what many small and struggling Cornish mines were like. It is also of a piece with another tale told locally
about Wheal Joney, "that the miners brought tin from elsewhere and propped it in position to convince the
captain to keep working it." (From Valerie Brokenshire's "A Village Portrait")*

During the 1870-73 tin boom there was some small
scale activity, after which the mine remained idle until 1881, when a little ore was extracted by a mine
captain and three assistants. This was probably
"Captain Joney". After 1883, the mine was not
worked again until 1889, when Captain Joney re-
sumed operations with an old man or two and a
couple of boys. To start with, he actually did cut
sufficient ore to yield 10 tons of black tin after
stamping at the King Stamps, but with the proceeds
from the sale of this he adjourned to the local
hostelry, the Britannia Inn. Soon he got fed up with
digging out tin, and thought of a little method of
whiling away the time more profitably, although he
did cut a little ore from time to time, to show there
was no ill-feeling. He advertised shares in the mine,
and arranged a very clever system to fool the shareholders. He kept one old man at the mine to tend
the engine, while two boys kept watch at the Nettles

Corner junction. The shareholders at this period
always arrived by Carriage, and as soon as the boys
saw them coming, one boy would run like fury up to
the mine to wake up the old man, to get the fires lit in
the engine-house, while the other would run for all he
was worth to the Britannia Inn, and rout out Captain
Joney, who took a short cut across the fields to the
mine, adjusting his collar and brushing his top hat as
he went. When the shareholders arrived at the mine,
after having wet their whistles at the Britannia, they
would find Captain Joney waiting to meet them, and
the engine-house chimney smoking cheerfully. After
they had departed, Captain Joney returned to his
normal habitat again. His activities earned the mine
another local nick-name - that of "Britannia
Consols", it being said that the inn ought to be one of
the mine's major shareholders. This state of affairs
lasted until 1893, when presumably the shareholders
must have got wise to him.

WALK 13
THE GOVER VALLEY

Under two miles if based on Trewoon.
About four miles if walked to and from the centre of St Austell.

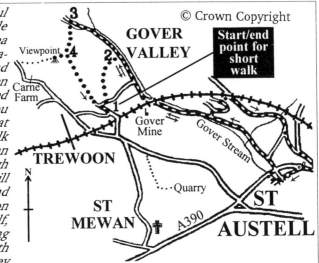

This is a beautiful and varied little walk in an area where old china-clay workings and quarries have been largely reclaimed by nature. If you start and end at Trewoon, the walk need take only an hour or so, although I think you will want to "stand and stare", especially on the second half, where the long views contrast with the wooded valley scenery that came before. Despite a fairly steep climb out of the valley, the walk is an easy one, if somewhat muddy at times. Trewoon has a pub and shops. Extending the walk to St Austell makes a pleasant addition. Recommended background reading for this walk is "Clay Country Remembered" by R.S.Best (Truran, 1986), one of the best-written (no pun intended) books of personal reminiscences I have come across.

Directions for a walk starting and ending at St Austell are given at the end. To base the walk on Trewoon, which is on the A3058 a mile or two west of St Austell, take the right turning soon after you enter the village, Trevanion Hill, which is beside the Trewoon Garage and Stores. Roadside parking should not be hard to find on this small estate, but please be careful not to block entrances. Western National bus services 21 and 22 link St Austell and Trewoon.

TREWOON

The name is basically the same as that of Troon, south of Camborne, meaning "the farm on the downs". Although the old spelling has remained in use here, "Trewoon" is pronounced almost as "Troon", but with a hint of a second syllable: "Trooan". The Manor of Trewoon appears in the Domesday Book as "Tregoin". The parish church, St Mewan, is about half a mile south of the village; the oldest parts are Norman, but the bulk of the building is 15th century, heavily restored by the Victorians. Obtainable in the church is J.B.Lamb's excellent booklet, *St Mewan - Saint, Church and Parish,* which contains interesting information about Trewoon and Polgooth as well as the church itself.

1 **Walk to the end of Trevanion Hill, which crosses the main London-Penzance line, and turn right on a minor road. After a short distance, take the footpath on the left, signed "Path to Gover".** This delightful path, sloping gently downhill, runs between quite high leafy hedges, but provides good views over the Gover Valley, in which the stack and roofless shell of an old china-clay dry (Forest Dry) make a prominent feature, overlooked by a shapely little green mountain. (This waste heap and the adjacent pit are known locally as "Teddy Bear", but I must admit I don't quite see the resemblance. Charles Thurlow suggests that the name may come from the nearby Trembear pit and hamlet.)

THE GOVER VALLEY

"Gover" simply means "stream", so the name on the map, "Gover Stream", is a parallel to such examples as "Pill Creek" and "Penare Point". For decades it has been known locally as "The White River"; it is, of course, a tributary of the St Austell River, which was also given that nickname while it acted as a drain for china-clay waste. Even now the Gover Stream is often a bit cloudy: a little way up the valley it flows through a small pond that looks like milk with a turquoise tint. During the 1860s there was talk of extending the Pentewan railway through the Gover Valley to thriving works like Halviggan, Forest and Greensplat: John Lovering, who then owned the clayworks called Carne Stents in the valley, wrote in 1864 that "it would be a great thing for the port of Pentewan, that it would take nearly all the clay in the valley, viz. from ten to twelve thousand tons." Unfortunately, sufficient capital was not available. The Gover Valley is known locally as "The Stents", presumably referring to Carne Stents. "Stent" in china-clay terminology normally means hard-rock waste, but in this case it may have referred to tin (Cornish, *stean),* because tin was a by-product at Carne Stents. A small mine in the Gover Valley also produced some tin: see the directions for the extended walk to and from St Austell. R.S.Best's book *Clay Country Remembered* (see the introductory note) mentions that some Carne Stents workers were the first to come out on the occasion of the china-clay strike of 1913. The china-clay enterprises in the valley seem to have closed down a good many years ago; the Gover Clay Co., for example, closed as part of a "concentration" scheme to conserve resources during World War II.

To the right is the railway viaduct, with "Brunel's stumps" alongside, and beyond that a glimpse of St Austell.

"BRUNEL'S STUMPS"

Isambard Kingdom Brunel's broad-gauge main line from Truro to Plymouth, known initially as the Cornwall Railway, required the building of 34 viaducts, so he devised a relatively cheap design often called the "fan viaduct", consisting of stone piers with a timber superstructure. "Spider bridges" was another nickname often used. Viaducts of that type totalling nearly four miles in length were built during the 1850s, and even more were added soon afterwards on branches such as Truro - Falmouth. "It is generally supposed," wrote Canon Hammond in his *A Cornish Parish* (1897), "that these wooden bridges are precarious, and there have been people who would not take the railway journey through Cornwall because of their supposed insecurity. I believe that they are really safer than iron structures." And a footnote adds, "This is true of the beams, but some of the stone piers are said to be shaky. One in the Gover Valley (so one of the engineers assures me) moves when a train passes over it." Although in principle the design was perfectly satisfactory, the timber proved very costly to maintain, so when the need became apparent for the main line to be doubled the task of replacing Brunel's viaducts with all-stone or brick ones (or embankments, in a few cases) was undertaken, starting in 1871 and not completed till 1934. The Gover Viaduct was replaced in 1898; so too was the one in the Trenance Valley, which is known as the St Austell Viaduct, presumably to avoid confusion with Treffry's Trenance Viaduct at Newquay. The new viaducts were built beside the old, so that there needed to be hardly any break in train services. Most of the "stumps" of the old viaducts are still in place; some stone from the stumps at Gover was, however, used in the building of Forest Dry. Charles Thurlow tells me that workmen were stranded for a while on the top of a stump when a falling stone smashed their ladder. A detailed and fascinating account of the building, maintenance and dismantling of the wooden superstructures is given in *The Centenary of the Cornwall Railway* by R.J.Woodfin (1960).

Soon, the path joins the entrance drive to a house named **Trevanion Mill Cottage**; nothing seems to be left of the mill itself apart from some ruined walls half-hidden by vegetation almost opposite the point where the path joins the drive. The house on the right at the foot of the drive looks quite new, but is in fact a converted chapel.

2 Turn left along the sandy track running up the valley, which soon passes a ruined cottage and the Gover Valley Kennels. The Gover Stream was quite fast-flowing, creating a series of small rapids, when we did this walk. At first, however, it can be heard but not always seen, as a result of the infestation of Japanese knotweed; and on the left are several rhododendrons of the rampant purple variety, *ponticum* - one of them determined to break into flower in late October! These, despite their beauty, are almost as serious a menace, since they create heavy shade, destroying smaller native plants that provide a much better wildlife habitat. **Ignore the right fork in the track.** The disused dry of Carne Stents clay works is on the left, but little can be seen from the track, apart from some high retaining walls.

Carne Stents secured a place in Cornish industrial history as the spark which ignited the Great Clay Strike of 1913. A demand by some 30 men for increased basic pay (from £1 to 25/- per week) and recognition of their union started a chain reaction which ended in a strike by the entire china clay industry workforce of 5,000, with police being drafted in from as far afield as Bristol and South Wales. After ten weeks of bitterness and violence the workers were defeated, but scarcely six months later the employers did raise wages to a level which, if granted earlier, would have made the whole sorry business unnecessary.

Further on, at the point where there is a five-bar wooden gate on the right, keep to the main track, which now leaves the Gover and follows a tributary that joins it from the west. On the right, near the gate, is a ruined building including two grates, the remains of another old dry.

3 When you reach a small group of cottages, cross the iron footbridge on the left. A flight of steps now takes you quite steeply up, and soon you have a good view over the valley. Continue uphill on this narrow path among gorse and brambles. Coming into view now behind are the huge spoil-heaps of the china-clay works in the Hensbarrow area; on the right, crowned by several circular settling or de-watering tanks, is St Mewan Beacon. **After the kissing gate, walk beside the hedge on your right.**

4 At the second kissing gate, where you turn left down a tunnel-like track past Trevanion Farm to return to Trewoon, you could first walk a little way along the track on the right which leads to **Carne Farm and St Mewan Beacon.** Since the hilltop itself is not accessible to the general public, it's probably not worth continuing to the road just below it, but I **would recommend going as far as the first gate on the left for the sake of the view.** Perhaps you'd like to test your own local knowledge by trying to name the most obvious landmarks, starting on the far right and working gradually leftwards: 1. the engine house with separate stack; 2. the village on the skyline; 3. another engine house on the skyline, this time with stack attached; 4. the deep valley leading down to the sea; 5. a third engine house, without visible stack, on a hill; 6. a church quite close at hand, its tower just visible among trees; 7. a small, ivy-covered stack on a hill, with a large waste heap on the right side of it. (You'll have done well if you know that last one, but all the others are visited or at least mentioned on walks in this book.)

ANSWERS

1. Ventonwyn Mine; 2. Sticker; 3. South Polgooth Mine; 4. the Pentewan Valley; 5. Taylor's engine house, Polgooth Mine; 6. St Mewan church; 7. Tregongeeves quarry, where there is a deep-looking flooded pit. A path leads up to the quarry from Meadow Park, the first right turning as you drive from Trewoon towards St Austell on the A3058.

TO START AND END THE WALK AT ST AUSTELL

From Fore Street walk down West Hill, a minor road starting at the roundabout opposite Globe Yard, which takes its name from a former coaching inn. Until 1833, when Truro Road was created, West Hill and Ledrah Road constituted the turnpike west from the centre of town. On the left are the Baptist Chapel and a former school, now part of the local College of Further Education. The northern terminus of the Pentewan Railway - see Walk 7 - was also on the left, lower down, near the three-arched 16th-century granite West Bridge, and one or two original buildings have survived; nothing remains, however, of the St Austell Foundry, which stood beside the railway yard, at the corner of Moorland Road: it was demolished about 1900. Its cast-iron nameplate is now at the Wheal Martyn Museum, at Carthew north of St Austell on the A391. Leo's now occupies the site of the old gas works, and Payless has replaced the workshops of the Cornwall Aviation Company. Cross the old bridge and turn right to walk beside the St Austell River. At the main road turn right, crossing the newer and much less attractive bridge, and turn left up Gover Road. Urban scenery soon gives way to suburban - and then rural, where the road narrows and the pavement temporarily stops. Now there is woodland on the left, and the Gover Stream becomes more obvious. Beyond the bridge the stream is on the right, and there are no more pavements, but the road is usually quiet at this end.

Very well hidden among trees, shrubs and undergrowth on the left just before you reach the viaduct is the engine house of Gover Mine. Its recorded output, covering the years 1858-1881, was mainly iron plus some tin. According to Dines and Collins the workings were opencast, and this would suggest that the engine was to work the stamps. Kenneth Brown, however, has been told that "the engine used to work flat-rods through the viaduct into an adit on the opposite hill."

After passing under the viaduct, continue ahead, ignoring the left turning to Trewoon. At the entrance to White River Cottage, on the right, you have a good view of the stack of one of the many small disused clay dries in this area. The path from Trewoon joins this valley road or track from the left at the drive to Trevanion Mill Cottage; pick up the directions at point 2.

To walk back to St Austell later: the "tunnel-like track" mentioned at the start of point 4 ends on the edge of the housing estate; there turn left along a minor road which brings you back to the Gover Valley. Turn right, and soon you are walking under the viaduct again.

Rather than simply retracing your steps along Gover Road, after about half a mile you could go left up Turnavean Road. Keep on that as it curves right and left, and immediately before the entrance to No. 42 go up the path on the right, between a wooden fence and metal railings. This brings you to Trenance Road, which you join beside a pair of railway bridges: the nearer one, with rather beautiful brickwork, is presumably the newer of the two. An old china-clay works (Trenance Dry) is perched up above the bridges, and just beyond them is a loading bay with a small chute. Turn right, down Trenance Road, for St Austell. Now you have good views of the Gover Valley and Viaduct, and finally the road sweeps down past more of "Brunel's Stumps" beside another grand railway viaduct, this time crossing the St Austell River, hurrying on its way to Pentewan. Trenance Road joins Bodmin Road, which soon returns you to Fore Street.

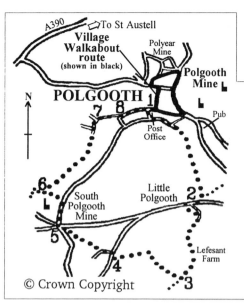

This is a pleasant short walk featuring attractive countryside along with plenty to interest the "industrial archaeology" enthusiast. The going is mostly easy, but mud is to be expected on at least one part of the route. Polgooth has a shop where you can buy provisions, and also a large, quite "up-market" pub well-known locally for good food. A short stroll round the village is suggested as a little "extra" in the note about Polgooth.

Polgooth is signposted from the A390 a couple of miles west of St Austell. The village streets are rather narrow, but roadside parking is usually possible near the post office. Alternatively you could, with permission, use the Polgooth Inn car park, though this tends to be full, especially at weekends.

POLGOOTH (with a short walk to explore the village)

The name probably means "goose pool", which perhaps implies a farming community, but for centuries life in the village was dominated by tin and copper mining (the latter mainly in the first half of last century). Nowadays its roles seem to be mainly as a dormitory for St Austell and towns as far away as Plymouth, a site for pleasant retirement homes, and a magnet for weekend visitors attracted by its very popular pub; but relics of the mining are by no means limited to the two ruined engine houses overlooking it from the east and the south-west. To see some of the others, I suggest a short stroll round part of the village not included on the main walk, as follows.

From the post office go down Fore Street (i.e. turn right if you were coming out of the shop). At the bottom turn left, soon passing the Manor House. On your right now is East Rand, mentioned in the note about Polgooth Mine; the stamps engine house is clearly visible, with its stack a little way up the tree-covered slope. At the corner with Trelowth Road was the main shaft of Polgooth Mine in the 18th century, and this is where the house built for the earliest beam engines would have been. A few yards past that on the left is a deep cutting, usually with pools in the bottom. This is in fact what in Cornwall was known as a "coffin" or "goffan" and in coal-mining country would be called open-cast mining; Hamilton Jenkin refers to it as "the great open-cut". It is presumably very old, probably pre-dating most of the shaft mining at Polgooth, and it provides a vivid illustration of one of the factors that made the mine so profitable, namely that many of the mineral lodes are at comparatively shallow depths. The coffin was once much longer than it is now: the far end of it has been filled in during recent years. (Not much further along the valley road is St Margaret's Holiday Park, where the engine-house of Polyear Mine is; it is not visible from the road, except perhaps in winter, so to inspect it you would need to seek permission from the owners.)

When you reach Trecarne Close turn sharp left up a path running beside Rosemellyn Holiday Bungalows (St Margaret's Lane) and bear left where that joins the slightly wider Stony Lane. This brings you back to Trelowth Road. Turn left to look at the Old Count House, not much altered since it was the administrative centre of Polgooth Mine. According to Cyril Bunn's *Book of St Austell*, "As many as 2,000 miners were paid from the balcony above the front door in the mining heyday of the village." Joy Wilson's *Around St Austell Bay* has a photo of the house when it was the home of a coachmaker and wheelwright. Follow the sign to the post office, going up the narrow road known locally as "The Nip", which starts beside the Polgooth Press premises. The building housing the post office is, we were told, one of the oldest in the village; it was originally a farmhouse and later became a school - hence the little tower. A photograph of Polgooth exists - though I haven't seen it - which was probably taken from Mulvra Hill (on the east side) in about 1910, soon after most mining ceased, and apparently it shows hardly any buildings except the Manor House, the Count House and what is now the post office. It would seem that many of those 2,000 mine employees (women and children included) must have walked considerable distances to work, or that their cob-walled cottages in the village must rapidly have returned to the mud from which they came.

1 **From the post office/store at Polgooth, take the side road (past the post box), and at the Polgooth Institute turn left.** You are now on Bal East Lane, a name which reflects the importance of mining to this village. On the hill ahead now, in the middle of the St Austell Golf Course, is Taylor's pumping-engine house, the most prominent relic of Polgooth Mine; and soon you get a view of another engine house, recently very imaginatively converted into living accommodation, in the valley below.

POLGOOTH MINE

Often referred to as Great Polgooth Mine, at certain periods it was called Polgooth United, Old Polgooth or Polgooth & Tregontrees. (So says Dines, though I wonder if it was really "Tregongeeves", the name of a nearby quarry and farm, and the home of Loveday Hambly, "the Quaker Saint of Cornwall" (1604-82).) "Old Polgooth" is certainly apt, because there is documentary evidence that shaft mining was being carried out here during the 1590s. The popular beliefs that it produced "the first tin in Cornwall", that tin from Polgooth was used in the building of King Solomon's temple, and that two tin ingots found in the Pentewan Valley nearby were dropped in the river by Phoenician traders - all these are rather more difficult to verify; in any case, tin obtained in medieval times or earlier would almost certainly have been "stream" rather than "lode" metal. (See the note on

Happy Union & Wheal Virgin Streamworks in Walk 7.) Celia Fiennes visited the area in 1695 and wrote, "There were at least 20 mines all in sight, which employ a great many people at work almost night and day, including the Lord's Day, which they are forced to prevent their mines being overflowed with water. More than 1,000 men are taken up about them ..." *(Through England on a Side-Saddle)*. She didn't name the mines, but they were almost certainly at Polgooth.

Before long most of the small mines had merged. In about 1720, Thomas Tonkin called Polgooth "the richest work this day in England or, I believe, that ever was in this Kingdom." At about the same time another writer referred to it as "this vast mine." In 1726-7 Polgooth acquired one of the first steam engines to be erected at a Cornish mine, a Newcomen engine with a 50-inch-diameter cylinder. A 63-inch Boulton & Watt engine replaced it in 1783. These engines were near the former count house, but as the mine developed more and more of the work was concentrated under Mulvra Hill, which divides the Polgooth and Pentewan Valleys; this area is especially rich in tin (plus some copper) because lodes running east/west intersect there with others running south-east/north-west. In *A Topographical & Historical Description of Cornwall* (published 1810), John Britton and Edward Wedlake Brayley stated that there were "not less than fifty" shafts. They described a "stupendous steam-engine ... which raises the water to the adit-level like the fountain of a river." For about fifteen years from 1807 the mine was closed (largely, it seems, because of disputes about smelting), but by 1823 it was under the management of John Taylor, who was at that time also breathing new life into the great Consols copper mine in Gwennap, and about to embark on the building of the Redruth and Chasewater Railway. The large engine house still dominating the area from the top of Mulvra Hill was built for an 80-inch engine capable of raising 1,000 gallons of water per minute: the second engine of such size to occupy the position. A smaller engine for winding was also erected on the hill, and a 25-inch stamps engine in the valley, linked to the working shafts by a tramroad with an inclined plane to the stamps. By 1837 Polgooth was reckoned to be the county's third largest producer of tin; but five years later it closed again because of low tin prices and from then on its fortunes were very chequered. In 1882 a larger stamps engine house was built, recently converted as a dwelling.

All mining below adit level at Polgooth had ceased by the start of this century, but from 1902 to 1929 a reasonable living continued to be made by Thomas Sweet, who extracted valuable metal from the old dumps and shallow workings and processed it in and around the stamps engine house. Having spent some years mining in South Africa, along with his four brothers, he named his enterprise "East Rand". His grandchildren, Brendan and Pauline, still live there, and have done much to preserve and restore the water-driven stamps and other equipment Thomas used. A photograph showing him and his workforce posing beside the stamps is on page 25 of Peter Bray's *Around & About St Austell, 1880-1930.*

A narrower path down to the left (at the point where the track curves right) would bring you to the Polgooth Inn, if you're ready for that so soon. The main track is tree-lined and has good valley views: pleasant walking. **After** less than half a mile it brings you past a bungalow and down to a road a few yards beyond that. (Ignore the signed footpath going left.)

2 Turn right on the road, and then almost immediately left; use either the concreted road or the rough track on the right of it: they soon meet again. The minor road now goes uphill past Lefesant Farm and then becomes a rough track, passing a converted farm building.

3 Be careful not to miss the right turning that comes quite soon, where there are a few steps down and then a muddy patch followed by a steepish, narrow path that is evidently used by horses. ("Muddy Lane" is the locals' name for it.) At the top you have a good view over St Austell, with huge china-clay dumps on the skyline. Continue ahead on a track, with another engine house ahead - that of South Polgooth Mine.

SOUTH POLGOOTH MINE

This was another ancient mine (its main lode, called Baldu or Baldue, is mentioned in a 16th-century document), but it never achieved anything approaching the size and prosperity of Polgooth Mine. Its deepest workings are only about 276 feet (46 fathoms, in the usual mining terminology). The engine house was built in 1880 for a rotary engine which was used both for pumping and to work 16 heads of stamps. The last active period of the mine was 1915-18, when arsenic was produced; the ruins can still be seen of the Brunton calciner, where ore was roasted, and the concrete-topped flue leading from that to the engine-house stack. For brief explanations of the processes involved in collecting and refining arsenic, and some comments about the uses to which it was put, see *The Landfall Book of the Poldice Valley* and *A Second View from Carn Marth*. A fascinating photograph of South Polgooth when it was producing arsenic is on page 50 of *Around St Austell Bay* (Bossiney Books). What an amazing transformation in less than seventy years!

4 At the road turn right, and after about 100 m. take the signed public footpath on the left, through a wooden gate. Quite soon (no more than 50 m.), cross the stile on your right, and go diagonally across the field, through the gap in the corner, and then walk beside the hedge on your right. Where that turns right, go straight on to a gate with a footpath sign. This brings you to a crossroads called Five Turnings.

5 Follow the sign to Polgooth. Just past the engine house, take the path on the left, which runs quite close to it. The mine buildings are surrounded by scrub, but there are one or two more-or-less overgrown, narrow paths which may enable you to take a closer look at them. If you do, please take great care, because they are in a fairly advanced state of decay. The ruined building with a corrugated roof on the left beside the track belonged to the mine and is said to have served as a carpenter's shop and miners' dry (changing-room). After the mine closed it was used as an abbatoir for a time.

6 To walk back to Polgooth, you could return to the road, but more attractive is to take the narrow path on the right just before you reach the wider track. On the right of it at the start is an old mineshaft. **Soon you will reach a wider path with hedges both sides, Higher Coombe Lane. Turn left on that.** It runs down into Polgooth, an attractive path if rather stony underfoot in places. Here and there you may notice boundary stones, because the lane marks the division between St Ewe and St Mewan parishes.

7 At the wide track turn right. The lane's name, Tyshute, may mean "house *(chy)* of the water-chute". Compare the Shute at St Day, which was till well into this century the town's main water supply: there are photographs of the water-cart being filled at it. The stream which may have fed the chute here appears from the OS map to emerge from a mine adit (drainage shaft), but this is something I have not been able to check.

8 At the road turn left to return to the post office.

WALK 15
ST EWE AND POLMASSICK

A little under four miles, or there are shorter versions.

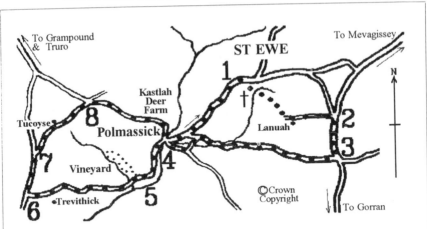

This short inland walk would be ideal for wet-weather conditions, because most of it is on minor roads; one section uses a field path and a farm track, but a route along roads could be substituted for that.

The main points of interest are two delightful and unspoilt old villages, one of which has a church well worth visiting; and a vineyard in a beautiful valley. The vineyard is open to the public during the season, and in addition to strolling around the grounds you can get refreshments there - and buy the wine. The countryside is very pleasing: rolling hills cut through with many little wooded valleys and studded with sturdy old farm buildings. Most of the farms have "diversified" to some extent - by offering holiday accommodation, for example, and in one case by stocking its fields with deer.

The walk is generally easy, but there is one quite long climb. A few short stretches of road are likely to be moderately busy at the height of the holiday season. Toilets as well as refreshments are available at the vineyard (Polmassick), and there is a very appealing pub at St Ewe. As this is a figure-of-eight walk, you could easily cut out half of it if you wish, for example by starting and ending at the vineyard, thus covering only sections 5 to 7 and the start of 8 in the directions.

The Crown Inn at St Ewe and the Polmassick Vineyard both have car parks for customers, and it is usually possible to park near the church, but in that case please try to avoid times of services. St Ewe, some three miles west of Mevagissey, is signposted to the right on the road from St Austell to Gorran; driving from Truro you could take a right turning on leaving Grampound and, with the aid of a map, approach St Ewe via Polmassick.

ST EWE CHURCH

When I taught at Falmouth School I
became acquainted with the eloquent
and erudite vicar of Budock, the Rev.
John Rham, now Canon Rham. The fact
that his previous incumbency had been
that of St Ewe appealed to my sense of
humour as much as to his own. I
wonder if it ever found its way into one
of those little books with titles like
Strange but True or *Funny Peculiar.*
According to Oliver Padel's *Cornish
Place Names*, St Ewe the person was
probably, as you might expect, female,
but that's about all anyone seems to
know. The name of the nearby farm,
Lanuah, means "St Ewe's church-place",
and it confirms that that saint's name
was originally two syllables, "Euwa" or
"Ywa"; the village name, however, is
locally pronounced "St Tue", and
appears in 16th- and 17th-century
documents as "Twe" and "St Tew".

The glory of the church is the intricately carved rood screen, said in
the church guide leaflet to be "the only one of its kind and age in Cornwall
to have escaped destruction by Cromwell's soldiers". It's a pity the church
is so dark inside that it's difficult to make the "close inspection"
recommended by the leaflet; John Betjeman lays the blame for that on the
much-maligned J.P.St Aubyn, who restored the church in Victorian times. If
you need help with interpreting the details on the screen, Arthur Mee's
Cornwall is a useful supplement to the church guide. In addition there are
several interesting monuments, a Norman font, an old wagon roof in the
south aisle, and old carved bench-ends incorporated in the pulpit. Ivor
Herring (see the note on Heligan, Walk 6) has made a copy of the 1676
seating plan, now displayed in the church. It is worth close study for the
light it sheds on Cornish society at that period. One interesting point is
that most, but not quite all, of the wives were segregated from their
menfolk in church. Mr Herring has contributed an interesting article
about this seating plan to the Autumn 1991 edition of *Old Cornwall.* He
also mentions that St Ewe is unusual among Cornish churches in having a
broached spire, that is, one where the awkward change from a square
tower to an octagonal spire is made by broaches (half-pyramids) at the
corners.

Near the gate is the tombstone of Hugh Atwell, rector of St Ewe (d.
1617), whose skill in "Phisike" (medicine) was commended by Carew in
the *Survey of Cornwall.* Even apart from the fact that "his iudgment in
urines commeth little behind the skilfullest in that profession", he was
unusual in prescribing milk and apples rather than relying on blood-
letting. Among many other virtues, Carew also praises his "liberalitie": "on
the poore he bestoweth his paines & charges *gratis.*"

1 From St Ewe Church, I suggest you start by trying the one part of the walk which may give rise to problems, namely the field path to Lanuah farm. You need good watertight boots for it unless the weather has been unusually dry, and at the very start you may need a stick to cope with nettles and other vegetation. *(If all that sounds too off-putting, you could instead walk east on the road towards Mevagissey; that is, from the church go past the pub. Ignore the left turning, towards St Austell, but take the first turning on the right, which comes after about a quarter of a mile. This minor road brings you to Beacon Cross; pick up the directions at point 2.)* For the footpath, walk through the churchyard on the east (left) side of the church. A path leads to the left-hand corner, where you may have to knock nettles aside in order to reach some steps that lead down to an old pump in a hollow. A couple more steps up on the other side of the hollow bring you to a barbed-wire fence, but you should be able to get round that to the left by pushing back a few branches. Step across the stream - I hope it won't be too wide for that - and go a few yards left to where it's quite easy to climb the far bank. Now walk up the field, just left of the top of the ridge. When the buildings of Lanuah come into view, head for the one furthest right. Go through the five-bar wooden gate, then walk up beside the hedge on your left and through another gate, where you turn left to pass among the old farm buildings, and continue ahead along the rather muddy farm lane to join the road at Beacon Cross.

2 Turn right there. (The reasons for the name are soon obvious: an ancient Cornish cross stands beside a small layby opposite, and the view eastward includes a long stretch of coast, with the daymark at Gribbin Head prominent, so presumably beacon fires were once lit here. The cross is described by A.G.Langdon in *Old Cornish Crosses* under the name of Corran.) This road can be busy at times, so please take care.

3 At the crossroads, where there are signs left to Kestle (one of seven Cornish places so named; it can mean "castle" or "fort", but might be just a "settlement"), turn right. This unsignposted back-road - no more than a lane - runs gently downhill most of its length, with a charming little valley to the left, and later it gives a good view ahead of Polmassick hamlet and the woods above it. You could take the even narrower road (known as Drunkards' Lane) on the left beside a bungalow called Sunny Corner (unless the name has changed now - always a danger when giving directions); this goes beside some derelict cottages. One of them is apparently being considered for restoration; called Bunny's Cottage, it is named after a "freelance" farmworker who is still remembered locally. Turn right at the T-junction, and soon you will reach the crossroads at Polmassick, where the River Luney passes under a pretty two-arched bridge on its way to the cove which bears its name, overlooked by Caerhays Castle. The name "Polmassick" means "Madek's bridge", *pons* having become *pol.* The name of one of the cottages shows that there was formerly a mill here.

4 You could return direct to St Ewe by turning right; but for the complete walk turn left, where a board announces Polmassick Vineyard.

Rather strangely in this lovely spot, the ground on the left has been allowed to become the industrial world's answer to the elephants' graveyard: a place where old lorries and JCBs come to die. You can soon forget that, however, as you turn up the short drive beside a converted chapel to the vineyard.

POLMASSICK VINEYARD

Described by its present owners as "Cornwall's first commercial vineyard", it was begun in 1978 when Müller Thurgau and Seyve Villard vines were planted. The first commercial crop (two tons) was harvested in 1983, and since then several other varieties of grape have been tried. At any time of year you can buy bottles of wine, but to tour the grounds, sample wines by the glass and get refreshments (mainly ploughman's lunches and cream teas) you need to come between the second May Bank Holiday weekend and the last Sunday in September, 11 am to 5 pm - not Mondays apart from Bank Holidays. One of the biggest attractions is the delightful little walk you can do: it runs near the bottom of a very pretty wooded valley, where a cow, a calf and a Falabella pony called Vino introduced themselves to us, and returns to the Winery at a higher level along a grassy track that is shown on some old maps as a road. Seats are strategically placed to help you to enjoy the views.

5 To continue the walk on leaving the vineyard, turn right and go on up the valley road. Kilbol House looked a delightful spot for a quiet holiday; so too in its very different way did Trevithick Barton, described as a 16th-century farmhouse offering en suite accommodation, which stands at the top of the long hill. The hedges are high up here, but a gateway on the left gives you a view of the coast, presumably at Porthluney.

6 At the T-junction turn right. Take care on this rather busy road.

7 Take the first right turning, signposted "Polmessick". Tucoyse ("woodside") farm is yet another which now caters for the visitors, the old barns having been attractively converted into "holiday cottages" in a pleasant setting, complete with duckpond. Tucoyse Manor is listed in the Domesday Book as "Ticoith".

8 At the T-junction turn right. From here you get a glimpse of St Ewe spire. The road descends back into the Polmassick valley, with tall trees overshadowing mossy, ferny banks which I would guess are smothered in primroses and bluebells earlier in the year. Towards the bottom of the hill you may catch sight of a few deer in the fields to the left, part of the herd of Kastlah Deer Farm. **At the Polmassick crossroads go left, following the signs to St Ewe and the Crown Inn.** Soon you have quite wide valley views to the left, and can get an impression of the size of the Kastlah herd. The stone and slate-hung houses and the deserted-looking farm on this side of St Ewe superficially appear to be older than most of the buildings close to the church; maybe that's why the latter have to proclaim their antiquity by their names: The Old Stables, The Old Pottery House, The Old School House ... Unfortunately, what might have been a useful shop is now The Old Post Office. Luckily the pub is just a few yards away. That's old too, and so is some of its furniture, especially the wonderful curved, high-backed oak settle beside the oak fireplace with its pewter pots and dishes. We found the menu good and the welcome friendly. The little building in the pub's car park was originally St Ewe's clink, where offenders spent the night before being taken to the nearest police station. The small square in front of the church was once the village market-place, and the stone centre-piece formerly served as a mounting block. The column at the centre may possibly be the remains of an old cross; it used to be crowned with a sundial.

St Ewe

WALK 16
COOMBE AND DOWGAS
Just over three miles

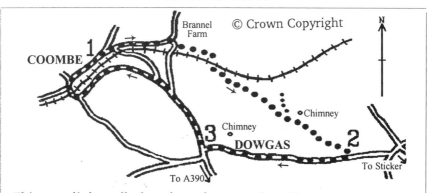

This easy little walk, based on the attractive village of Coombe, runs through an old tin-mining area on the southern edge of "china-clay country". Old shafts, overgrown burrows (mine dumps), several stacks and an engine house are on or close to the route. This is remote-feeling countryside whose peace is rarely disturbed except by the occasional train on the main London - Penzance line, which is close at hand during most of the walk. The paths and tracks used on the first half of the walk are likely to be muddy in places; the second half is on minor roads which seldom see much traffic. Most of the road walking is along a ridge which gives wide views, especially to the north. A couple of gates will probably have to be climbed. There is no pub or shop on the route, but a diversion would enable you to visit Sticker, where there are a shop and the Hewas Inn, an attractive pub with an interesting and very reasonably-priced menu. This, however, would add at least a mile and a half of road walking, so you might prefer to call there with your car, as we did, when the walk had given us a good appetite.

Coombe is a mile or two south of St Stephen-in-Brannel, and quite easily accessible from both the A390 and A3058 roads, but you may find it helpful to refer to a fairly large-scale map. Coming from the A390, if you enter the village by going under the railway bridge on the south-west side, turn right there, following the sign to High Street and Lanjeth, through the main part of the village, and if possible park beside the road somewhere before the first turning on the right, or not too far beyond it.

1 To start the walk, take that right turning, which runs gently uphill, still mostly among the trees that help to make Coombe so attractive. Strictly, its name is St Stephen's Coombe, to distinguish it from the many other Coombes in Cornwall. (There are at least two within five miles of my own home - one on a creek of the Fal and another between Bissoe and Cusgarne - and both are beautiful spots, like this one.) Like the Welsh "cwm" it simply means "valley", or more accurately "small valley", in contrast to "glynn", "large valley". **Ignore the right turning, into a housing estate. When you reach a grassy triangle with a signpost left to High Street and Lanjeth and an unsigned road to the right, continue more-or-less straight ahead along a track** which makes pleasant walking but may be muddy at times.

The impressive farm buildings a little way off to the left are those of Brannel Farm, where quite a large area is devoted to rose growing. Brannel or Bernel was a Domesday manor, and the parish name includes that of its principal manor in order to distinguish it from the two other St Stephens in Cornwall, those "by Launceston" and "by Saltash". The manor house itself was at Court, a little further north than the farm.

Close by on the right is the railway line, but it is on a higher level and you may not be aware of it unless a train passes. Soon, however, the track takes you under a railway bridge. Then turn left, still keeping near the line at first. On the skyline to your left now is the massive Blackpool china clay works. **Ignore the bridge over the railway: go through the farm gate ahead and walk up the rather muddy little lane between hedges which soon brings you to Lower Dowgas farm**, complete with thatched farmhouse and two Shetland ponies. I'm not sure how permanent a feature the ponies are. **Continue ahead along the obvious grassy lane**, and soon you are passing among old shafts and waste-heaps, now mostly shrouded in thick vegetation - relics of St Austell Consols Mine.

ST AUSTELL CONSOLS

This was made up of several small old mines, at least one of which (Wheal Unanimity) was at work in the 18th century; others were called Hawkins and Trewithen, and East Wheal Strawberry was formed in 1835. The group, together with part of Great Dowgas, became St Austell Consols in 1844, and in 1864 the depth of the workings reached nearly 500 ft. During the 1860s engine houses for pumping, winding and stamps were built. In 1873 another company, St Stephen's Tin and Copper Mines, took over parts of the sett, but this seems to have been short-lived. Hamilton Jenkin tells the story of "a Mr Bargett" who in about 1907 hunted for nickel in the waste-dumps of this mine and "stored his finds in a nearby shed. At a later date the shed was removed and its contents thrown back on the burrows whence many good specimens of the ore were subsequently recovered by mineral collectors." Apart from nickel, tin and copper, the mine has also produced some uranium and cobalt.

Ignore the right fork. Where the grassy track curves sharply to the right, go through the wooden farm gate on the left or over the stile near it, and turn right on the stony track. You should now be close to a tall chimney, and soon a side-track to the left allows you to take a close look at it. It belonged to a beam engine used for driving the stamps at St Austell Consols. Close to the stack on the west a square depression in the ground marks the site of the boiler house. **Still continue along the main track,** among more mine workings, including a shaft on the left surrounded by a low wall. **Somewhere near here, according to the OS Pathfinder map, the right of way diverges to the left from the**

main track, but we failed to find it, so unless it is reinstated at some future date walkers have no choice but to continue along the track - and that appears to be the right of way according to the Landranger map. Go through the wooden farm gate, then past an old building on the right, now in agricultural use but probably, in Kenneth Brown's opinion, originally the mine's smithy. The metal farm gate (padlocked when we did this walk) brings you to a road.

2 **Turn right on that.** *If, however, you want to include a visit to the pub and/or shop at Sticker on the walk, turn left and then take the second turning on the right. After about half a mile this brings you to the former A390 (now bypassed) just beside the pub. Return the same way.* This minor road runs almost due west, giving you good views to the right across the mining territory you have just walked through, to the distant china clay tips, with the village of Nanpean on the skyline. On the ridge to the left is the engine house of Ventonwyn mine, with its separate stack.

VENTONWYN MINE

The stamps engine house of Ventonwyn is among the best-known in the county, being a very dominant feature, especially to those driving towards St Austell on the A390; and it shares with several other famous ones such as Wheal Coates near St Agnes the dubious distinction of having been built for a comparatively unsuccessful mine. Originally called Wheal Elizabeth, it was, as Dines puts it, "worked in a small way for many years", but the only recorded output is of 138 tons of black tin between 1903 and 1907, which is when the stamps engine was used. The name, meaning "white spring" or possibly "beautiful spring", is that of a nearby farm.

Just beyond Dowgas House is another lone stack, this time belonging to the arsenic calciner of Great Dowgas Mine. An unusual feature of the chimney is that even the top part is built of stone: normally brick was used because it was more convenient for the tighter circle and thinner wall as the stack tapered.

GREAT DOWGAS MINE

The name, "Dowgas", is from the Cornish *dew cos,* two woods. There's not much woodland at Dowgas now, and perhaps the mines are largely responsible for that: huge quantities of timber were consumed by mining, especially in order to supply charcoal for smelting in blowing-houses. By 1719, however, Great Dowgas Mine was sending tin to the smelting house at Calenick, south of Truro, one of the earliest to use the new "reverberatory" furnaces, which burnt coal and anthracite instead of wood and charcoal. (See Walk 12 in *A Second View from Carn Marth.)* Like Polgooth Mine (Walk 14 in this book), Great Dowgas was fortunate in working lodes some of which were at shallow depths, and as at Polgooth much of the earlier mining was by means of an open cut. (The most famous example of this form of tin mining was at Carclaze, north of St Austell, whose impressive pit attracted many visitors. By 1850, according to one estimate over a million tons of ground had been excavated There is a brief note about Carclaze in Walk 12.) What Hamilton Jenkin calls "quarry-like excavations" on Goffan, Goffins or Great Stopes Lode at Dowgas were still clearly visible when he was writing *Mines and Miners of Cornwall* during the 1960s, but they were filled in about ten years ago. During the 19th century, deeper mining was carried out. Hamilton Jenkin tells the remarkable story of a group of six men who in 1828 took only six weeks to sink a shaft of 222 ft; their pay totalled £40, and for that they also excavated the plat and erected a horse-whim! (Sorry about the technical terms ... a plat was a flat area, in this case for the horse-whim, a capstan-like structure used for winding and turned by literal horse-power.) The same George Henwood I mentioned just now referred to the "Hot Lode" at Great Dowgas, saying it was one of the hottest in Cornwall: "the roof and sides of the workings are studded with minute crystals and efflorescence from the decomposing iron pyrites, the heat from which cause is so oppressive that a visit of a few minutes is all that can be safely endured." The mine continued to be worked for both tin and copper at various periods during the 19th century, and its last period of activity was from 1905 to 1913, in conjunction with Ventonwyn Mine. Details of this final working, together with four photographs which show how much has changed in 80 years, are in the 1985 issue of *The Journal of the Trevithick Society.*

3 At the crossroads turn right. Ahead now in the middle distance is the tower of St Stephen church, with a backdrop of china-clay tips. **Either of the two right turnings would bring you back into Coombe, but to avoid covering again some of the ground you have already walked ignore those and continue on the "main" road as it curves downhill and then runs beside the railway line, finally passing under the bridge beside Coombe chapel.**

Great Dowgas, with the huge waste tips of Blackpool china clay pit beyond

WALK 17
ST STEPHEN-IN-BRANNEL, COOMBE, RESUGGA CASTLE AND TOLGARRICK
with a possible extension to GRAMPOUND
A choice of routes ranging from about 5 to 10 miles

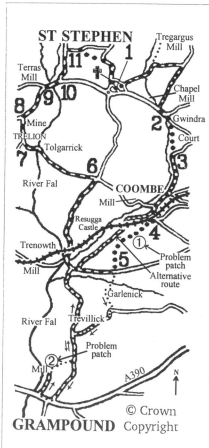

This walk has great industrial archaeology interest, featuring mines, railways and especially china-stone grinding mills. It links with the next one, because both follow the course of the River Fal, and Resugga Castle is part of the same system of Iron Age settlements and fortifications as Carvossa and Golden Fort. The walk includes a fine medieval church, a museum of motoring and attractive countryside, with many old bridges and former watermills. The area is not much frequented by walkers, it would seem, and we did meet problems, notably at the points marked (1) and (2) on the map, so before you set off I suggest you check my comments about these in the directions. Some sections of path are likely to be muddy. Much of the route is on roads - quiet ones, apart from a few yards along the A3058. There are pubs and shops at St Stephen and Grampound. If you like to take your own picnic food with you, Resugga Castle would make a pleasant spot to eat it: a picnic table is provided, the views are good, and it's a real sun-trap on warm days. It has a car park, and would therefore make a good alternative point to start and end.

The directions start at St Stephen church. There is a car park by the recreation ground near the churchyard. Two pubs, the King's Arms and the Queen's Head, are near the church, and both are well-recommended for their food. I can personally vouch for the pasties at the King's Arms: genuinely "home-made", and even the "small" ones are a good plateful. We haven't used the Queen's Head, but I hope soon to investigate David Guthrie's remark in *Cornish Pubs:* "The pickled bums are remarkable and stimulate conversation." They are not, I presume, on the menu.

ST STEPHEN-IN-BRANNEL

The name of the local manor (sometimes found in other forms: Burnel, Brenel, Branel, Branwell ...) is added in order to distinguish this parish from two others in Cornwall, although in fact they are both called "St Stephens": one at Launceston, the other near Saltash. "The name Brannel is thought to mean corn ground," says *The Cornwall Village Book,* but Oliver Padel says it is "unexplained".

St Stephen-in-Brannel has an attractive nucleus of granite and slate terraced houses with two pubs and an old school building clustered around its fine medieval church. As a market village it has a long history (and a colourful one: the sale of a wife for 4d at St Stephen market in 1835 recalls the opening of Hardy's *The Mayor of Casterbridge,* and the fictitious wife-sale happened at about the same date); but its growth to the status of a small town (population now about 2,000) began with William Cookworthy's discovery in about 1750 "that in the neighbour-hood of the parish of St Stephens, in Cornwall, there are immense quantities of both the petuntse stone & the caulin". "Petuntse" and "caulin" (kaolin) were his versions of Chinese words; the English equivalents are "china stone" and "china clay". The landscape to the north is now dominated by great china-clay works; in contrast, the china-stone industry has declined, but relics of it still exist within and all around St Stephen, even on the southern side, which at first sight seems utterly rural. (See the note on Terras Mill.)

Before Cookworthy's time, in fact, such industry as there was in St Stephen parish consisted mainly of tin streaming in this area south of the village; there were also a few small metal mines one or two of which became quite important during the 19th century and continued working into the 20th.

The brothers Silas and Joseph Hocking were sons of the owner of one of these mines; both were ordained Methodist ministers, and between the 1890s and the 1930s both became famous as the authors of literally scores of "healthy" novels carrying the Methodist message. Silas in particular achieved best-seller status, and Arthur Mee claims that he was the first writer ever to sell a million copies of his books in his lifetime. Now the Hockings are almost forgotten (though a biography of them by Alan Kent is in preparation), but a nephew of theirs born at nearby Goonamarris, the blind and almost deaf poet Jack Clemo, has achieved a literary reputation that will surely last, however minute his sales may have been in comparison with theirs. He died at the age of 78 in 1994. His novel *Wilding Graft* gives a vivid and completely unglamourised picture of life in and around St Stephen (and also in Truro) during the late 1930s and early '40s. St Stephen's claim to a share in the glory of the Brontë sisters is a little more tentative: their mother was Cornish, and her surname, Branwell, suggests that her forebears hailed from this parish. In the world of sport St Stephen men have made a name for themselves in Cornish wrestling and especially tug-o'-war. (The Terras team of 1914-37 was particularly celebrated, according to a newspaper article John Yeo showed me.) Finally I must mention the achievement of a miner at the Victoria Inn, St Stephen, reported in *The West Briton* in 1844, who "ate half a pound of candles for a wager of a quart of beer. This done, he offered to eat another half pound for a further two quarts."

ST STEPHEN CHURCH

Although it lacks the beautiful carving of Probus and St Austell churches, St Stephen's does not lag far behind them in terms of generous size and pleasing proportions. The church lies in a hollow, but its tall tower commands a fine view. (Incidentally, Dr John Penderill-Church's book about William Cookworthy tells - perhaps with a grain or two of poetic licence - how he climbed the tower to survey the scene in his search for china clay, and thus found his way to Carloggas, about a mile to the north-east, where a small tin mine had created a white scar ... From that discovery flowed many changes for the people of this parish.)

As mentioned elsewhere, there is some evidence that an earlier church was sited further east, but the existing building dates at least from Norman times: the larger font at the west end is said to bear carved portraits of William the Conqueror and his queen, along with what John Betjeman calls "Tiger Tim". The south door, with its unusual "nail-head" ornamentation, is the other notable remnant of the Norman church. Most of the building, including the tower, is the work of the 15th century. When the church was restored in 1854 it was less drastically Victorianised than many in the county. Much of the early woodwork has gone, but the wagon roof in the north aisle is original, and old carved pew-ends were used in constructing the pulpit.

Under the floor of the Lady Chapel is the vault in which the Tanner family, Lords of the Manor of Brannel, were buried. The story is often told of how, when the vault was opened at the time of the restoration, the coffins were found to be unusually large - some over seven feet long. According to the church guide leaflet, descendants of the Tanner family on a visit from New Zealand in 1960 remarked that their own 13-year-old son was already over six feet tall; and the anonymous author of the piece about St Stephen in the WI's *The Cornwall Village Book* (1991) says that the present occupants of the manor-house site (Court Farm) are also exceptionally tall. One stained glass window at the east end of the church depicts china-clay working.

The churchyard has a small Cornish cross, brought here from a field at Treneague Farm. The church guide suggests it may date from about the year 200, although Arthur Langdon in his book on Cornish crosses argues that no Christian cross in Cornwall is earlier than 5th century. Near the cross is a pillar sometimes called the "Reading Stone" or the "Crying Stone", because it is said that in the days before newspapers the latest news was announced here after Sunday morning services.

1 From the main church gate, opposite the King's Head, walk through the churchyard, continuing ahead past the church to the gate at the far end. Turn right at the road, then left at Trevear

Road. Soon you cross the bridge over a stream which will accompany you on much of the first half of the walk.
Where the road bends quite sharply right, a track on the left beside houses gives access to a beautiful wooded valley and the ruined china-stone grinding mills of Tregargus and Trevear. Despite the neglect these have suffered since they fell out of use in the 1960s, they are still a fascinating and impressive monument to this once-important industry (some details of which are given later, especially in the note on Terras Mill), and the imaginative use that was made of water power calls to mind such places as Kennall Vale and the Luxulyan Valley. One big waterwheel was saved from destruction, but is now in an advanced state of decay. A brief description of Tregargus Mill, with two photographs, is in *Industrial Archaeology of Cornwall* by A.C.Todd and Peter Laws (1972). In Alan M. Kent's novel, *Clay* (Amigo Books, 1991), Ben brings his girlfriend Chloe to this place. "She loved it down there," Ben remarks; but he "did not tell her that a man was killed here once under the weight of the massive grindstones. It would have ruined the picture for her, taken away the romance of the mill." From what I have been told locally, the "man" was little more than a boy, who, like many others, enjoyed taking rides on the merrygoround ... There is no public right of way in the valley: the site is still a registered quarry owned by English China Clays International and part of it is leased to the Goonvean and Rostowrack China Clay Company, which uses the old quarry pit above the mills for dumping. ECCI will probably grant permission to organised groups wishing to visit Tregargus (or Chapel Mill, mentioned later).

Continue along the road past Trevear (or Treveor) Farm - notice the mullioned windows of the farmhouse - **and at the T-junction turn right. After about half a mile you reach the main road, A3058. Cross with care and turn left; luckily you don't have to brave the traffic for many yards.**

2 Where the main road curves left, take the right turning, signposted Langerth and St Stephen's Coombe, and then cross the stile immediately on your right. The path now keeps fairly close to the stream on your right and takes you down this attractive valley. It is historically interesting for several reasons. Tin-streaming was carried out here: in 1780 streamers found two pieces of worked gold which may have been prehistoric, together with coins from the reigns of Edward III and Henry II. Shaft-mining also took place nearby, and the OS map marks an adit (drainage shaft) emptying into the stream from the high ground to the west. The mine, which seems to have produced little if any metal, was called Gwendra or Gwindra, which is the name of the farm on your left, now the site of a small industrial estate; but another name for the mine was Egloshellen, from another nearby farm, nowadays usually spelt "Eggloshellans". *Eglos* is a Cornish word for "church", so it seems probable that the original Celtic church was in this valley. A Cornish derivation of "hellen" seems possible: *hen-lann,* old cemetery; but Oliver Padel agrees with the church guide in suggesting a dedication to an unknown Celtic saint. Certainly the chief manor of the parish was here, the Manor of Brannel, which was probably the Domesday Manor called Burnel. Up on the left after you have passed through a kissing gate is Court Farm, which occupies the site of Court, the manor house, records of which go back at least to the 13th century.

Its last occupants were the Tanner family, about whom there is a comment in the note about the church. The manor house is said to have been destroyed during the Civil War. (Brannel, further south, was the manor farm.) In the distance ahead on the skyline is the stack of Ventonwyn Mine (the engine house is less clearly visible from this angle). **The valley path ends rather muddily at a stile, beyond which is the entrance to Bodinnick Farm, and then comes the road.**

3 Turn right there, still with the stream on your right; the wooded ground on the left is the site of old quarries. **Soon you are entering Coombe village.** The name of the first house shows that the stream has, or at any rate used to have, the same nickname as so many others near St Austell: the White River. Sometimes still it looks rather milky. Its official name is, I gather, the St Stephen River, though I have also heard it called the Wheal Arthur River, at least in its upper reaches near the old mica works of that name. The decrepit little waterwheel beside the house is another reminder of times past: Mr Jack Goldsworthy tells me that to his knowledge at least 27 waterwheels were powered by this stream alone. **Continue past the playing fields and through the village** - a peaceful spot in a pretty setting, though it seems a pity that so many characterless modern dwellings have been allowed to crowd around the original buildings such as the "Old Sunday School Cottage". **Ignore the right turning, to St Stephen and Newquay (although you might care to go a little way up there to see the remains of Coombe Vale Mill on the right - another china stone mill); go left at the next junction, and under the railway bridge.**

4 Turn right immediately, following the footpath sign. The path runs beside the main London-Penzance line at first and then curves left, uphill. **Soon another path crosses it, and here is the first of the "problems" I mentioned in the introductory note, marked (1) on the map. The right of way continues straight ahead, but there is a barbed-wire fence across it. A proper stile is needed, but meanwhile a makeshift "stile" suitable for reasonably agile walkers is on the right, where it's possible, if you walk round to the right-hand side of the tree there, to climb on to the stump of a bough and hop over the fence; failing that, you may be able to duck under the wire a little further to the right, near an old gate.** *(If, however, you find you cannot manage it, an alternative route using a minor road is available, as shown on the map. Return past the shop and turn left. After nearly a mile, at the T-junction turn right, and pick up the directions at line 8 in section 5.)* **After the barbed wire, continue uphill for a few yards on the line of the path by which you came, and then go diagonally right to the top of a small wooded or scrubby patch, where there are several clear paths running parallel.** From here you get a good open view dominated by the huge waste tips of the Blackpool china-clay works; and then ahead you see the main line curving below in quite a deep valley. The hill on the far side of that is crowned with a circular field: this is Resugga Castle, details of which are given in a later note. From this vantage point it is particularly easy to appreciate how strategically placed the fortification was. **Go through the**

metal farm gate up on your left. Now keep by the hedge on the right at first, and then after the wooden farm gate curve left to a concrete reservoir, where there is another wooden gate. Go down the tractor track, which brings you to a road. The big house ahead is Garlenick.

5 Turn right at the road, *but if you want to extend the walk to Grampound, fork left immediately, taking the track to Garlenick. Directions are given at the end of the main walk. Please note that "problem patch (2)" is in this section.* For the more direct way back to St Stephen, continue along this pleasant, quiet, wooded road, which passes Treway farm (shown as "Mill" on early OS maps) and descends gradually to the valley of the River Fal. Ignore the first right and left turnings, but turn right after crossing a bridge (over the St Stephen River), following the sign to St Stephen.

First, however, I recommend a short diversion: cross the second bridge, a two-arched one, which takes you over the Fal, and continue along the road. After yet another bridge you come to a nicely modernised former corn mill which till recently was in use as a pottery. On the left nearby, still fairly complete but now mostly hidden among trees, are the remains of Trenowth China-Stone Mill. Return the same way.

The road to St Stephen takes you past the beautifully-situated Crow Hill Cottage with an old dry opposite (which dried the stone ground at the Coombe Vale Mill), under the viaduct and then quite steeply up Crow Hill.

This is another area of historical interest. Habitation in ancient times is suggested by the discovery by tin-streamers nearby of an ornamental brass/bronze collar dating from about 100 AD. The viaduct, known officially as the Fal Viaduct, was rebuilt in 1884. Only one "stump" seems to remain of Brunel's original viaduct, which like all 41 other viaducts on his Cornwall Railway had a wooden superstructure. For some details about the old "fan viaducts" and their replacement, see the note about the Gover Viaduct in Walk 13. The filled-in brick arch on the right as you pass under the Fal Viaduct may be another relic of the original structure. The rough ground on both sides of the road was mined, mainly for lead, silver and iron: H.G.Dines gives details of Crowhill and New Crowhill Mines, which worked at various times between 1853 and 1913. Up on the right are what Barry Atkinson describes as "a very smally-constructed engine house, the stump of a stack and a burrow" (waste tip); unfortunately, he adds that they are "best viewed from the Trenowth railway viaduct", so watch out for them when you next cross that! The engine house was built for a 12-inch all-enclosed beam engine (like the one at Levant, recently restored by the National Trust and the Trevithick Society), used for winding; the pumping was done by waterwheel. This mine is supposed to have produced some uranium (see the later note on South Terras Mine).

Among the woods on the far side of the Fal is Trenowth. Like most of the many other places in Cornwall called "new farm", this one is very old: the manor of "Trefneweth" was given by King Edgar to one of his thegns in 969. Several chapels at Trenowth were licensed for worship in the 15th century, and the ruins of one of them were "still clearly visible" when Henderson was writing, probably during the 1920s: the Pathfinder map indicates "Chapel" among the trees beside the Fal. Trenowth House itself, I believe, dates only from the 1930s.

At the top of the hill, turn right at a wide, gravelled entrance and go through a wooden kissing gate to explore Resugga Castle.

RESUGGA CASTLE

The name derives from the Cornish ros-googoo, "hill-spur of the cave or hollow". Just where the cave or hollow is or was I don't know: possibly nearer to Resugga Farm, about a mile to the north. Like Carvossa and Golden Fort (both a short way south, and both visited on Walk 18), Resugga Castle is a Celtic Iron Age hill fort, and the closeness of all three to the Fal suggests the strategic and commercial importance of the river during the four or five centuries before Christ. Resugga's site, on a spur above the confluence of the St Stephen River and the Fal, is clearly ideal for guarding trade routes and sources of stream tin. The main enclosure, surrounded by a rampart about nine feet high and a ditch about three feet deep, is D-shaped and about 120 yards across at its widest point. On the right side of the car park as you face the earthwork is a sunken entrance trackway which passes between two outlying ramparts; these may be relics of an annexe to the main fort, possibly for the corralling of cattle. Incidentally, the 19th-century OS maps indicate another, smaller, earthwork named Burghgear, "the house of the fort or round", a short way to the south (surprisingly, not on the main spur opposite Resugga but on the slope south of Treway farm). There is no trace of it on the modern maps.

Continue along the road as before. The long, low modern building ahead, on the edge of St Stephen, is Brannel School (comprehensive); on the skyline are good examples of both types of china-clay sand tips, the conical "sky-tips" and the "finger-tipping" which, being much safer and more practical for large volumes of sand, has now superseded it. The tips you can see ahead are at the Melbur, Virginia, Treviscoe, Goonvean and Trethosa works, and Blackpool is to the right.

6 At the crossroads, for the shortest way back to St Stephen continue ahead; but for the full recommended route, turn left, following the sign to Trelion (pronounced as per the animal's name, and sometimes spelt "Trelyon"). **Before long this road descends to the Fal valley at Tolgarrick Mill,** presumably a corn mill, but little if anything seems to have survived in recognisable form. From the bridge over the Fal can be seen an old stack, a few yards up-river, and beside it are the overgrown ruins of a mine's treatment plant. This is a relic of the most important mine in this area, South Terras. **Continue along the road.**

SOUTH TERRAS MINE

The first recorded output of South Terras dates from 1873, but how much earlier than that work started is not known. It began as an iron mine, producing also a little ochre and tin; along with these the miners found a mysterious mineral (actually torbernite) which they nicknamed "Green Jim". ("Jim" was a reference to James Harris-James, the mine's managing director/agent.) In the early years this was hand-picked, packed in barrels and exported to Germany for use as a pigment in glass and black porcelain. In 1889 J.H.Collins was asked to inspect the mine, and the contents of his report were, as he puts it in his *Observations on the West of England Mining Region* (1912), "boomed in the newspapers throughout Europe and the United States for all they were worth, and more." "This lode," he says in the same book, "is certainly one of the most important deposits of uranium ores yet discovered anywhere in the world." And in a footnote he adds, "I say nothing of its radium content, as I have no special information thereon; but it has been stated that contracts have been made for the supply of radium in large quantities."

Radium was discovered by the Curies in 1898. It is often said that Mme Curie visited South Terras as a possible source of radium for medical purposes, but there is no evidence for this belief, and Courtenay Smale (who has made a close study of the mine's history) is very sceptical about the story. What can be established is that Mme Curie's Preparator carried out sampling at the mine in 1912. At about that time the French Société Industrielle du Radium took over the mine, but the war put a stop to its work. A radium-extraction factory which was set up after the war closed in 1929. ("Production of radium bromide often averaged a tenth of one gramme per month, about the size of a pin head," wrote Mr Smale in an article for the *West Briton,* 10.8.95. "In the 1930s," he added, a bizarre scheme to turn South Terras into a radioactive health spa came to nought.") At the time of the Hiroshima atom bomb, the *News Chronicle* featured on its front page a claim that the uranium used in it came from South Terras, but Mr Smale has dismissed this idea.

H.G.Dines's account of the mine in *The Metalliferous Mining Region of South-West England* ends, "Attempts were made to sell the tailings as radioactive manure." In the good old academic tradition, he resists any temptation to add an exclamation mark. The Cornwall Heritage Project's booklet, *China Clay District Driveabout,* points out that another radioactive element discovered by Mme Curie, polonium, was also produced at South Terras, and that "weight for weight it is a hundred thousand million times more toxic than cyanide gas." (Polonium and actinium cake was, Mr Smale tells me, sent to the Continent, mixed with glycerine and used as a relief from rheumatism.)

The miners worked only during the summer because so much water entered the workings at other times; even so, I wonder about the life expectancy of the men who ate their croust amidst the Green Jim and grew the spuds and turnips in their pasties with the aid of that manure ...

7 At the T-junction turn right. This hamlet, consisting of little more than a few cottages, some of which have now been merged and christened "Tinners House", is called Trelion, meaning "farmstead of the flat stones".

8 At the next T-junction again turn right, and soon you reach a converted engine house, now called "Stack House". The rotative beam engine which it had held stopped working about 1906, and even before it was removed for use at a china-clay pit the building had been bought for domestic conversion: "a possibly unique instance," Kenneth Brown tells me, "where the roof, door and window joinery were retained for the dwelling and did not accompany the engine to its new home." The engine house was built by a small enterprise called Terras Mine.

Now the road descends gradually, with the pleasant countryside of the Fal valley to your right. The ground on both sides was worked by Terras Mine for tin during the 1870s and '80s, mainly by means of open cuts.

9 At the main road (A3058) turn right - but first have a look at the big old building on your left, rather patched and dilapidated and partly adapted for use as a greengrocer's-cum-florist's shop, but still of considerable historical interest. This is Terras Mill.

TERRAS MILL AND THE CHINA-STONE INDUSTRY

St Stephen china stone, a partially-decomposed form of granite, has long been recognised as a useful building material. Charles Thurlow tells me he has noticed at least 35 references in *Lake's Parochial History* (c.1870) to the use of "St Stephen granite" for carved features inside churches. Probus church tower is probably built of it, as well as the one at St Stephen itself; so too is the tower at St Columb Major, and William Cookworthy's discovery of this fact in 1748 was one reason why he turned to the St Stephen area in his search for good-quality materials for the manufacture of ceramics. With the rapid growth of the china-clay industry from the late 18th century onwards increasing quantities of the stone were quarried. Ground to a fine powder and mixed with china clay, it acts as a flux in the firing of porcelain, and (to quote William Cookworthy's patent of 1768) "gives the ware ... its transparence and mellowness." Several mills were built in and around St Stephen, employing waterwheels to drive grinding pans, the bases of which were made of china stone. A mixture of water and small lumps of the stone was fed in, and revolving arms propelled big blocks of china stone on top of it, creating a white "mud". John Yeo, the owner of Terras Mill, showed me where a leat once brought water from the River Fal; the wheelpit made for a waterwheel built at the Bartle Carn Brea Foundry in 1898; the low building housing the grinding pans; and the settling-tanks where the process of drying the "mud" began. All this is behind the big building with its rust-gaudy corrugated roof, now in use as a shop and store. Until about 1934 this was the mill's kiln or dry, built like a china-clay dry with linhay (storage area - pronounced "linny") alongside the drying pans: the remains of its stack can still be seen at the far end, and the fire grates were just to the right of the present shop as you enter. The building was used as stables for about ten years from 1945, and relics of this episode in its history are still clear to see. Terras Mill may not be among Cornwall's architectural gems, but I wholeheartedly support Mr Yeo in his determination to resist tempting offers from "developers" with plans to beautify it - or, more probably, replace it with yet another housing estate. As far as I know, no grinding of china stone is done in Cornwall now, and only one company continues to quarry it: suitable types of feldspar, which is the important constituent of china stone, can now be obtained more economically abroad, for example from Canada and Scandinavia.

The ruins of another china-stone mill in St Stephen are beside Hawkins Motors, on the A3058 a few hundred yards west of point 2 on the map. This was Chapel Mill, an interesting name because no-one remembers a chapel on this site, but Henderson notes that the area was named as "Chapel Park" (=field) as long ago as 1578. Although at first sight little besides the stack seems to have survived, Charles Thurlow and John Hawkins tell me that there are three grinding pans, a waterwheel, leats and other remains. The possibility of visits to this site by organised parties is mentioned in section 1.

To continue the walk, procede with care a short way along the main road, crossing the Fal at Terras Bridge. "Terras" may mean "three fords", and a glance at the OS map shows that there could well have been as many as that at this point in the valley.

10 Take the first left turning, which soon brings you to the "Automobilia" Motor Museum, housed in what was a working corn mill until Worls War 2. Even if old cars don't interest you, you may well be glad of the chance to visit the museum's snack bar. Opening hours are 10-4 in April, May and October, and 10-6 from June to September.

Continue along the road as before. What appears to be a long, low hill on your left is in fact a waste tip for fine sand and mica residues from china-clay workings. The OS map describes the area as an "Experimental Seeding Ground", and evidently the experiment has been very successful. Some details about modern techniques of fertilising and seeding the steeper slopes of old tips are given in the Cornwall Heritage Project's booklet, *China Clay District Driveabout*.

11 Turn right. The road runs uphill through attractive, rolling country-side (mainly sheep-pasture, apparently), and soon brings you to Treneague Mill (pronounced "Trenayg"), with its attendant farm buildings and cottages. Treneague was once the site of an old chapel, and an ancient Cornish cross was found in one of its fields: see the note about St Stephen church. **Take the signed footpath on the right (to Trethosa Road). The path leads you through three kissing gates (though the second has almost gone, and the third is much patched), and then around the new primary school. At the road turn right. This soon brings you down to St Stephen church.**

EXTENDING THE WALK TO INCLUDE GRAMPOUND

This makes an attractive addition, but the suggested return route includes near the start a neglected short section of footpath likely to be very wet; as it's also steep, many walkers will feel unable to tackle it. To avoid it you would need to retrace your footsteps most of the way back.

   Starting at point 5 in the directions, take the track down to the mansion called Garlenick or Garlinnick. The full meaning of the name is not known, but Padel suggests the first syllable probably derives from Cornish *cor,* a hedge or boundary. He does not refer to the "ker" or "gear" (fort, round) shown on the old maps just to the west: see the end of the note about Resugga Castle. **After crossing a stream - much frequented by ducks - the track curves right beside the house,** looking rather like a cross between a Victorian school and a castle, **then left past cottages and farm buildings. After a farm gate you are on the main entrance drive, passing through Garlenick Woods. At the road turn right**, soon passing the restored former farmhouse of Nantellan. More attractive old farm buildings - and these still in use for farming - are on the right as you reach a T-junction; this is Trevillick. **Turn left at the junction,** and soon you pass Higher Trevillick. After that there are few buildings for half a mile or so till **the road becomes Pepo Lane and descends into Grampound.** It reaches the main road beside St Nun's Church, the market hall and the old cross-shaft: see the note on Grampound and other details about the village in Walk 18. **Turn right, past the pub, and continue till you reach Mill Lane, on your right, which comes shortly before the River Fal bridge. Turn up this road.** After several new houses, you will pass the surgery on your right, followed by small "cliffs" created by quarrying. The surgery occupies the site of the former village poor house, and it is believed that there was once a lazar house there or nearby. (For some information about leprosy in Cornwall, see *Around Looe, Polperro & Liskeard,* pages 18-20.)

   The large old buildings ahead and to the left at the end of the road are or were Grampound Town Mills. This grist mill is described by D.E.Benney in *Cornish Watermills* (1972); he traces its history back to 1607 and remarks, "It is indeed a rarity to find a watermill three and a half centuries later still operational and prospering." At the time he was writing, one of its two waterwheels had recently been renovated, although electricity was by then powering the mill. According to Amy Blane, however, writing 20 years later, the mill "has not been in working order for about twenty-five years" (*Grampound with Creed,* 1992). An overshot wheel remains, she says, "now rusted and certainly not in use". Unfortunately, little if anything of the mill itself can be seen from the road.

Follow the footpath sign (to Trevillick), which takes you under a building into what looks like part of the quarry. The path goes up steeply on the right: this is problem-patch (2). There is a rather rickety metal handrail on the left side of the path for the first few feet. In summer the path can be rather overgrown, and at all times it is likely to be very wet underfoot; indeed, in winter the path can turn into a stream or mini-waterfall. Even then there is usually just about enough stony bank beside it to make it passable, but obviously you need to proceed with great care. Beyond the small metal gate things improve, though cattle tend to churn up the mud in this patch. Ignore the obvious path up the field, keeping to the dip: go up to the top left corner, where there is a stile to the road by which you came down to Grampound earlier. Retrace your steps now till you reach the two Trevillick farms. There continue ahead, following the sign to St Stephen. Notice the small stone arch built into a barn wall at Trevillick, on the right beside the road. According to Charles Henderson's notes on Creed parish, it is inscribed "Found at St Naunter W.P.", referring to a chapel and holy well of St Naunter which once existed on the left side of the road about a quarter of a mile further along. The road runs through lush, rolling, wooded countryside with the River Fal down to the left and little besides the occasional farm vehicle on the road or train in the distance to break the silence. **At the T-junction turn left, picking up the directions at line 8 of section 5.**

Grampound

WALK 18
TREGONY, CREED, GRAMPOUND, TREWITHEN AND GOLDEN

About 8 miles.
A walk of about 5 miles omitting Tregony is also suggested,
and another of about 4 miles covering Tregony and Golden.
A further possibility would be a 3-mile walk including only Grampound
and Trewithen.

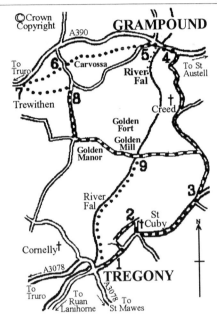

Despite nearly a mile on an A-road, this is a strong candidate as my favourite walk in this book: not only is the countryside beautiful, but there is an exceptionally high level of historical interest, plus the opportunity (except on Sundays and from October to February) to visit one of Cornwall's great gardens. Most of the route is on minor roads or well-made tracks, so it would be a good choice during a wet spell; the only likely trouble-spots from that point of view would be on the path beside the River Fal. The terrain is quite hilly, but the walk is not strenuous. Shops, tearooms, restaurants and pubs are at Tregony and Grampound, and there are public toilets at Tregony.

For the 8- and 4-mile walks I suggest Tregony as the starting point, because parking is comparatively easy there, and by beginning at Tregony you get the main-road walking out of the way quickly. For the 3- and 5-mile routes you will probably need to park on a side-road in Grampound; or if you are including a visit to the garden and/or house at Trewithen you may be able to leave your car there while you do a walk, provided that there is not too much pressure on the quite small car park.

1 **Walk up the wide main street of Tregony, past the King's Arms and Tregony Methodist Chapel. Immediately beyond that, turn left (toilets here) and then right, opposite the entrance to Tregony Holiday Park.** Notice the old pump. The little road lives up to its name of Back Lane by showing you the backs of the cottages and houses along the main street, and also of the primary school. Soon you come to Tregony Church.

TREGONY

Unusually, the name is stressed on the first syllable; a spelling of it from about 1540 is "Tregny". Polsue's statement in *Lake's Parochial History* that the Romans built a castle on the high ground overlooking the point where the stream on the south side of Tregony joins the river is no longer accepted. A century or more after the Norman Conquest, however, the manors of Tregony became the property of a family called de la Pomerai (otherwise Pomeroy), and they built a house on that site which seems later to have developed into a castle. Under their influence the small community rapidly gained status. Tregony Bridge was built, thus effectively cutting off Grampound from navigation; a new parish was created, a new church (St James's) was built just above the bridge, and a Priory was established beside the castle in the 13th century. The right to hold fairs and markets was granted, and also, at certain periods, to be represented in Parliament. (In 1620, when it was Incorporated, Tregony became a "pot-walloper" borough with two MPs, in which the right to vote was given to householders with a hearth big enough to boil a pot of a certain size on. This was one of the abuses ended by the 1832 Reform Act.) Several profitable woollen mills operated in and around the village, and in 1631 Tregony had 36 alehouses. All this prosperity was, of course, dependent on the success of the port, and by the 16th century that was seriously threatened, mainly because of silt resulting from tin-streaming. Despite at least two dredgings of the river during Henry VIII's reign, the quays became unusable, and St James's Church was abandoned by 1538 because the river kept flooding the low-lying ground on which it was built. *Old Cornish Bridges* by Henderson and Coates (1928) has a fascinating account of abortive attempts late in the 17th century to make the Fal navigable again as far as Trenowth (north of Grampound - see Walk 17) by a system of sluices and locks. The decline of the river trade and of places like Tregony continued; indeed, one settlement called Sheepstall or Sheepstores, a mile below Tregony, once the site of a market, chapel and leper-house, disappeared completely. The building of Sett Bridge at Ruan Lanihorne in the 1880s marked the recognition that navigation on the upper reaches of the Fal was finished for ever, and then as more and more silt from the china-clay district flowed down the river, Ruan too became inaccessible to vessels of any size. "The ugly white river of Fal discharges its burden of sand and gravel," wrote Henderson and Coates; compare the White River at Pentewan (Walk 7), which now, like the Fal, runs clear again. A walk round Tregony now reveals nothing of the castle, priory or St James's Church, and even the old bridge has been replaced; but the beautiful, wide main street hints at former glories, and there are interesting old buildings such as the two-storey almshouses known as The Gallery, dated 1696 but heavily restored about a century ago. They were originally described as "a hospital for decayed housekeepers".

The Church of St Cuby the Abbot is the original mother-church. A Celtic church, little more than a wattle hut, was probably built on the site in the 5th or 6th century, and the earliest parts of the present building date from the 11th century. As mentioned above, a new parish of Tregony was formed from part of Cuby in the 13th century, but less than 300 years later its church of St James was destroyed, and its congregation began walking

up the hill again to the old place of worship. In 1828 and again in 1899 it was almost completely rebuilt, so that the south porch and the 14th-century tower are almost the only medieval work remaining, apart from the beautiful 12th-century font. There is, of course, a great deal more to see than I have mentioned, and I strongly recommend the church guide, which includes scholarly and fascinating accounts of the life of St Cuby and the history of Tregony.

2 Turn right, and then left along the main road. There is a pavement as far as the Roseland School (comprehensive); after that you will need to walk on the right to face the oncoming traffic. I apologise for having to include main-road walking, which is never pleasant, but this is not usually very busy, and visibility is generally good. The entrance to Tregonhayne marks roughly the half-way point.

3 Soon after the right turning to Govelly, cross and turn left for Creed Church. This very minor road - little more than a lane - gives you, despite the high hedges, a good view ahead across the china-clay district, and at the top of the first slope a panorama on the left which includes glimpses of Creed church in the valley and the top of Probus church tower on the skyline to the left, beyond the woods of Trewithen.

A few yards past the right turning to Halbote and Bohago Farms, you could turn left on the grassy track and continue ahead to just below Golden Mill, returning to Tregony from there by taking the path on the left beside the Fal as described in point 9.

Continuing towards Grampound, the road descends to a pretty valley, crosses a small stream which I shall mention again later, and then comes Creed church, among nicely-restored old farm buildings. The River Fal is just below, and you can walk down to it if you like, keeping just left of the hedge or trees at the bottom of the graveyard. (The Trewithen Estate gamekeeper told us that there was once a bridge here or close by, and that the path continued up to Trewithen House, enabling the Johnstone family to walk to and from church; unfortunately it now stops dead at the river.)

Something about the setting of Creed church reminds me of St Winnow, despite the fact that the Fal hides away so shyly here, in contrast to the wide sweep of the Fowey there; but perhaps in reality it's only peace and beauty that the two have in common. (And holiness? I'll leave others to judge that.) Tybesta was one of the seventeen manors that made up the Cornish part of the Duchy of Cornwall when it was created in 1337, and Creed was its church. Its dedication is of special interest to my wife because she was born at Crediton, whose name apparently derives from the same female Irish saint, Credie. Most of the building dates from the 14th and 15th centuries, although there are a few small relics of the Norman structure. The restoration of this church, carried out in 1904 under the patronage of the "Squire" of

Trewithen, was much less harsh than most 19th-century restorations - in fact, as Betjeman puts it, "It is refreshingly unrestored"; and I would add, almost as delightful inside as out. The typed sheet available in the church usefully lists nine interior features in particular to look for. Two I would especially pick out are the inclusion of leather tanning among the carvings on the table to the right of the altar (a tribute, presumably, to the tannery in Grampound), and the photograph and other details near the organ about the discovery in 1791 by a Rector of Creed of Titanium, originally called Manaccanite because the sample of sand in which it was found came from Manaccan, near Helford. Not mentioned in the list, but worth a look, is the Parish Bier, last used in 1963. A placard explains that three teams of six men used to share the work of bringing it and the coffin from Grampound.

Back to the road, which now climbs out of the valley. At the top of the hill a right turning leads to Manheirs, one of several Cornish farms whose name refers to a prehistoric longstone: compare Tremenhere near Stithians, for example (*A Second View from Carn Marth,* Walk 8), where a menhir still stands. From here you have a view over Grampound, with Grampound Road on the skyline. Now the road widens. Notice on the right a wooden post with the base of a cross in front of it. Charles Henderson states that this is a relic of one of four crosses erected in this parish during the 15th century, perhaps to mark a place "where dead bodies are rested on the way to their burial - that prayers may be made and the bearers take some rest." As you enter Grampound you pass a former chapel of the Bible Christians, dated 1881, now converted into a private house. (For some details about the best-known of Cornish Bible Christians, Billy Bray, see Walks 1 and 4 in the book I have just referred to, and *Exploring Cornwall's Tramway Trails* Vol. 2.)

4 At the main road in Grampound turn left to continue the walk, but first it's worth turning right to look at the many interesting features of that end of the village, including St Nun's Church beside the small market hall with its clock tower.

GRAMPOUND

Its name betrays its origin: the "great bridge" was built during the 13th century at what was then the lowest bridging-point on the Fal. A document of 1299 refers to the "Borough of Ponsmur", which is the Cornish equivalent. The bridge itself was apparently never very impressive, and the "grand" presumably indicates its importance to the main trade- and pilgrim-route through south Cornwall. The old bridge, enlarged in 1782, was demolished in 1834 and a new one built a few yards to the north to carry the new main road: see point 5 in the directions. The bridge was further widened in 1969.

Official status as an incorporated borough came in 1332 or 1333: this conferred some tax exemptions and the rights to hang thieves and to hold weekly markets. In the 16th century the right to send two MPs to Westminster was granted. Grampound became perhaps the most notorious of all the "Rotten Boroughs" when the buying of votes there was cited by Lord John Russell as a prime example of electoral corruption; as a result, Grampound ceased to be represented as early as 1821, whereas other Rotten Boroughs survived until the 1832 Reform Act.

Because Creed church is so far away, there has been a Chapel of Ease in Grampound since at least 1370; it was dedicated at various times to St Mary, St Barnabas and St Naunter. After the borough was disenfranchised and lost its mayor and corporation the chapel fell into ruins; some of the old stonework, including a fine rose window, was acquired by Samuel Trist in 1827, and built into the entrance lodge of his new vicarage at Veryan a few years later. In 1869 a new chapel was built and dedicated to St Nun. St Nun or Non was the mother of St David of Wales, and her name also appears in that of Altarnun, on the edge of Bodmin Moor. Beside the chapel stands the 15th-century Pentewan stone market cross.

The little clock tower of the market hall (or town hall - on the site of the ancient guildhall) is a reminder of Tregony, and the comparison helps to highlight the urgent need for a bypass here. To me, in fact, it seems even more urgent than it ever was at Probus and Sticker, but at the end of 1996 it looks further off than ever. Instead, a traffic-calming scheme is proposed, involving speed cameras, rumble strips, "dragon-teeth" road markings, a narrower cariageway and a parking area, plus gateways at both ends of the village.

Then on the right come the two old houses called "The Manor" (possibly 15th-century in origin), with the Manor Tannery next door.

This is Cornwall's last remaining tanyard for the making of heavy leather - and yet Grampound alone had at least five tanneries in the mid-19th century. An interesting article about it by Byron Edwards in the November 1991 issue of *Cornish Life* claims it to be "one of the only two oak bark outlets in Britain, possibly Europe". (The other British one is in Devon.) Much of historical interest remains at the Manor Tannery, but unfortunately it is not open to the public for visits, partly because of the dangers involved. A detailed account of its history and the processes employed, with many photographs, is *Oak Bark Tanning in Cornwall* by Mary Cowan Doxsee; this seems to me to deserve publication, but at present is available only at the Courteney Library of the Royal Institution of Cornwall, Truro. The tannery achieved some fame when its leather was used in the construction of Tim Severin's curragh, "Brendan", which sailed from Tralee in May 1976 and reached Boston more than a year later, tracing the route thought to have been taken by an early Irish saint. William Croggon is quoted in the *Cornish Life* article as saying, "We quite deliberately use traditional methods of tanning to produce very specialist leather. While everyone else is aiming to get cheaper and cheaper, we have found a niche in the market for really top class shoes. These shoes sell all over the world and some of the highest in the land have our leather under their feet." The

Croggon family have been involved in tanning since 1712; *croghen,* by the way, is the Cornish word for "skin", but Mr Croggon assured me this is mere co-incidence: the family name was originally "Caroggon", and the Caroggons were farmers.

Almost opposite the tannery is The Hollies, the house just beyond the newsagents of the same name. It belongs to the owners of the tannery, and has an unusual garden of almost two acres, occasionally open to the public. For details see the current Gardens of Cornwall Open Guide, or you could enquire by telephoning 01726-882474.

Returning down the street now, if you call at the Dolphin Inn do have a good look at the wonderful old photograph of Grampound hanging over the fireplace. It was taken about 1900, and shows the children of the village lined up across the street, which sems to be surfaced with mud and has no traffic except one horse and cart; otherwise, little seems to have changed in nearly a century. (The same picture is in *Victorian and Edwardian Cornwall from Old Photographs* by John Betjeman and A.L.Rowse [Batsford, 1974].) Opposite the pub is the 17th-century Cottage Restaurant, where you could get light refreshments; a little further down the hill is a teashop (Perran House, on the right); and beyond that is Eastern Promise, a Chinese restaurant which attracts custom from far and wide: excellent if you want to give yourself a treat *after* the walk! Just past the junior school is the bridge over the Fal, an earlier version of which gave the village its name; but nowadays I suspect that most motorists and even some pedestrians cross it without noticing.

On the left immediately beyond the bridge is a footpath that runs beside the river for about a quarter of a mile; it would make a pleasant little diversion. There is some talk of extending the path further south to Golden or west to Barteliver, but at present it's a "no through road".

5 Go a little further along the main road and take the left turning signed to Barteliver and Golden Mill. At once you are among attractive old cottages. **Don't follow the road round to the left at Glenview, but keep straight on past more pretty cottages. The road soon becomes a track running almost due west along a ridge parallel with the valley where runs the A390,** glimpses of which you may occasionally get. The track you are on is shown as the only road linking Grampound and Probus (and therefore St Austell and Truro) on the OS map of 1813; the new road was built in 1834, so the ancient ridgeway turnpike road was superseded at about the same time as the earliest tramways (railways for horse-drawn wagons) were being laid in Cornwall. Just how ancient it is can be deduced from the fact that it runs right beside an ancient earthwork, Carvossa. This is easily recognised by the clump of trees just after the turning to the farm of the same name - not quite, as you might expect, at the highest point on the ridgeway, which comes a little later, where a road crosses. The northern ditch and rampart are very obvious, on the left close to the track.

CARVOSSA

This Iron Age settlement was taken over by the Romans (it may be the trading settlement referred to by Ptolemy as Voliba). Excavations in 1968-70 produced evidence that between about 60 and 130 AD its population outgrew the original oblong enclosure, some of them setting up home in the outer ditch or beyond. The main entrance was on the east. In addition to the ridgeway that still skirts the northern edge of the earthwork, there was a road running south-east from it to the Fal. A possible meaning of the name is "bloody (or bleeding) castle"; that's something to set your imagination working!

6 At the road, EITHER turn left for the more direct way back to Tregony, picking up the directions at point 8; OR go straight on along the ridgeway, here signposted as a bridle path to Probus, if you want to visit Trewithen Gardens and/or House (see the note below for opening times). **Where the main driveway curves left to Trewithen Farms, continue straight on.** Soon you have a view of Trewithen House left; and **finally the old road regains its original status by joining the modern A390.**

7 Here turn left along the main drive to Trewithen.

TREWITHEN

The name refers to the woods surrounding the mansion (Cornish *gwyth,* trees), which is basically 17th-century, but was greatly improved after 1715 when the estate was bought by the Hawkins family. Trewithen has a double link with Walk 7: firstly because the house is constructed largely of Pentewan stone, and secondly because the Hawkins family was responsible for building Pentewan harbour and railway. The grounds at Trewithen were much improved by Thomas Hawkins ("Squire" from 1738 to 1766) and some of his successors, but the beauty of the garden was created largely by George Horace Johnstone, who inherited the estate in 1904. If you would like to know the history of the house, the garden and their owners in more detail, see the excellent video film which is shown every hour on the hour during the garden's opening times: every day except Sundays from 1st March to 30th September, from 10am to 4.30pm. Dogs must be on leads. The house is open to visitors from 1st April to 31st July on Monday and Tuesday afternoons, 2 - 4.30pm, and also on August Bank Holiday Monday at the same times. (To check details for the current year, see the Gardens of Cornwall Open Guide.)

Following a visit to the gardens, **continue in the same direction past the house and a small lake; ignore the left turning (to the nurseries), and go on through the park to the road, where you turn right for Golden and Tregony** *(or left and then immediately right to return to Grampound via Barteliver, completing the 3-mile walk).*

8 Continue south along this pleasant country road and take the left turning signposted to Golden Mill. Almost at once you come to Golden Manor, on the right, with the farm buildings opposite.

GOLDEN MANOR

Although the name seems appropriate for this charmed spot, it is in fact thought to be a corruption of the name of the family that owned it until 1514, the Wolvedons. In that year it became the property, through marriage, of the Tregion family (pronounced "Trudgeon"). 63 years later, disaster came upon them when Francis Tregion was found to be sheltering a young Roman Catholic priest, Cuthbert Mayne. The latter was hanged, drawn and quartered at Launceston, and one of the "quarters" was put on display at Tregony. His head decorated the gate at Launceston Castle for a while, and part of the skull was preserved at Lanherne (see Walk 2 in *Around Newquay)* as a holy relic. Eventually, in 1974, Cuthbert Mayne was canonised by the RC Church. Tregian forfeited his estates and spent 24 years in prison. Finally he was released - by personal order of Queen Elizabeth, according to Norden - but had to live within five miles of the Fleet Prison. At last he was permitted to leave the country, and he died in 1608 at a Jesuit house in Lisbon. Tonkin states that in later years local people would show visitors the place where the priest was hidden, "under an old tower".

The most intriguing building is the ancient cowshed on the left, known as Golden Barn, which has a sundial and most of the external features you would expect of a medieval chapel, and "Chapel" is what the OS map labels it. Inside there is a spiral staircase. Charles Henderson writes interestingly about this barn in his notes on Probus parish, concluding that it was "probably the mediaeval house itself", and is likely to have had an oratory on the upper floor. Nigel Thomas (Cornwall Archaeological Unit) refers to it as a "medieval first-floor-hall house", and tells me that most of it was rebuilt last century, with various details from the original building used as decorative features.

The barn at Golden

Golden Keep, the older part of which, Mr Thomas says, may have been the first brick building erected in Cornwall, was restored during 1996. Roughly where the road bends right is the site of Golden Well, described by Meyrick as Holy and "an ancient stone structure in need of attention". Although very close to the road (on the right) it is not visible from it, and it stands on private land. So too does Golden Fort, on the hill to the left, and you would need permission from the Trewithen estate to go up the path to it.

GOLDEN FORT

This hill fort, often referred to as "The Warren", is in many ways similar to Carvossa, though it is larger, slightly different in plan, and had its entrance to the north-west. Like Carvossa it was taken over by the Romans and was conveniently situated at or near the tidal limit of an important trading river. Golden is another fort often held to be Ptolemy's Voliba. There are in fact six possible candidates in the Grampound area, and it could even be that all of them together made up the trading settlement given that name. Some scholars have suggested that "Vol" is an early version of "Fal", but that theory appears to be undermined by the fact, mentioned earlier, that the river seems to have been called the Cenion in Roman times.

There is no need to feel too frustrated, because the road down to the Fal is delightful enough in itself. The farm buildings near the bottom of the hill are called Golden Mill. There's no sign of a waterwheel now, but a legal document dated 1637 refers to "both mills at Golden". Golden Mill was certainly working by early Tudor times, because a bond was lodged during Henry VIII's reign for the building of a weir to improve its performance. For fuller details about the mill's history, see D.E.Benney's *Cornish Watermills.*

9 As soon as you have crossed the bridge over the Fal, to complete the 8-mile walk starting at Tregony take the path on the right that runs beside the river.

(Or, for the 5-mile walk starting at Grampound, go straight on through the farm gate, and keep to the obvious track up through the fields - ensuring, please, if you have a dog with you that it is fully under your control. At the minor road described in section 3, turn left for Grampound.)

This walk down the wide valley is probably the most attractive part of a route that was already full of delights; and still, as when we were on the farm track that was once a main road, we are reminded of the surprising changes that time brings by this modest watercourse that was once used by cargo vessels. In fact, even some of the tributary streams were navigable if the historian Norden is to be believed. Writing in about 1584, he says, "below Probus church is a rock called *Hayle-boate-rocke,* wherin to this day are many great Iron rynges whereunto Boates have been tyed: Now noe show of a haven, but a little brooke runneth in the valley." "Hayle-boate-rocke", explained by Polsue as "the rock to which boats were hauled", is presumably preserved in the name of Halbote farm, and the little brook that runs through Halbote is probably the one you crossed just south of Creed (point 3). (It's possible, I suppose, that the "little brooke" is the Fal itself, and Henderson and Coates in *Cornish Bridges and Streams* seem to assume that "Halbot" or "Holbert" rok was in the Fal.) **The path runs through woodland for a while and crosses a tiny stream; you have a wooden fence to** climb, unless you lower the removable bars (please replace them if you do); and then the path runs beside a hedge on your left, a bit further from the river at this point. At the section where it becomes a grassy track and goes slightly uphill you may encounter some muddy patches. The OS map shows a path through the marshy area near the river, reaching the road beside Tregony Bridge, but we kept to the main one which runs past a row of cottages (Mill Lane) and along Frog Lane to the main street.

The wide main street of Tregony. Repairs needed for the clock tower, along with the provision of an automatic winding mechanism for the clock itself, are estimated to cost £12,000. The village is hoping for help from the Millennium Fund to finance this.

Coffee stop overlooking Porthbean Beach (Walk 1)